# Clifford Goldstein

# FALSE BALANCES

# Clifford Goldstein

# FALSE BALANCES

**Pacific Press Publishing Association**
Boise, Idaho
Oshawa, Ontario, Canada

For Z.C.

Edited by B. Russell Holt
Designed by Dennis Ferree
Cover by Mark Stutzman
Typeset in 11/13 Century Oldstyle

Library of Congress Cataloging-in-Publication Data:
    Goldstein, Clifford.
    False balances: the truth about the judgment, the sanctuary,
and your salvation / Clifford Goldstein.
        p.        cm.
    Includes bibliographical references.
    ISBN 0-8163-1052-1
    1. Sanctuary doctrine (Seventh-day Adventists) I. Title.
    BX6154.G63      1992
230'.6732—dc20                                          91-17541
                                                        CIP

92 93 94 95 96 • 5 4 3 2 1

# Contents

# Introduction

A Christian-baiting university student from a secular Jewish home, the author of this book came to meet and know Jesus Christ as his personal Saviour through an extraordinary series of circumstances. Clifford Goldstein has seen God lead him in a most direct and remarkable way, despite a somewhat circuitous spiritual pilgrimage. The first steps of that journey he recounts in his autobiographical work, *Bestseller*.

As with other Christians, Goldstein found his difficulties did not come to an end when he became a Christian. He attended a major Seventh-day Adventist college in the early 1980s—just in time to catch the brunt of the heated theological controversies sweeping the church in those years. Strong winds both for and against the church blew against him there, but through his personal study, Goldstein came to have increased confidence in the special prophetic message the church is preaching today. He has presented his confidence in that message in his book, *1844 Made Simple.* Its clear explanations of complex topics have caused me to recommend the book to groups I have lectured to on this subject.

There is a third step in Goldstein's spiritual pilgrimage. It is not enough to begin the Christian life. It is not enough to have an intellectual knowledge of the Bible and its prophecies. Theology and doctrine must reach deep into our lives and affect how we live. That is the subject of this present book, *False Balances.* Here Goldstein deals with the major aspects of the Christian's spiritual life and the experience of salvation.

Unfortunately, it is precisely at this juncture that many Christians have difficulty. Salvation comes to us from a righteous God. He provides His righteousness to us through the vicarious, substitutionary death of Jesus on the cross as an atonement for all our sins and for the sins of the whole world. This is absolutely essential in the Christian life; no one can be saved without it. This precious gift must never be minimized or slighted. It must not be abused to provide a license for sin ("just come back to the well again and again").

There were those in the apostle Paul's day who misunderstood and misused Christ's work on the cross in such a way as to distort its true place in the Christian life. Sadly, the same is true today. In the book of Romans, Paul declared emphatically that we should never use God's wonderful gift of salvation as an excuse to break

His law and sin all the more. We may call those who hold this distorted use of the cross the "justification party" because of their emphasis of that aspect of salvation.

Others err in the overemphasis they place on the other side of the Christian life—sanctification. Hence, we also have the "sanctification party." This group tends to turn the Christian life into a matter of actions by which one attempts to deserve God's approval.

Godlstein argues that there is a true, balanced view of the cross and the work that was accomplished there. He also points out that it is not surprising that the Adventist Church today continues to experience such tensions. They have existed throughout the Christian church in all times. *False Balances* does an excellent job of pointing out the flaws in both of these extreme approaches to the Christian's life and experience with God.

But the book does more than point out problems. It calls for balance. We cannot afford to fall off the path to either side. Goldstein believes that the Bible itself points us to the very balance we so desperately need. He finds this balance in the book of Leviticus and the sacrificial system through which ancient Israelites received salvation. Goldstein finds justification and sanctification blended in the sanctuary. God called the Israelites to holy living on the basis of the gracious gift He had provided in the sacrifices. Justification thus becomes the motivation for sanctification.

Goldstein finds the same balance at various points in the New Testament. Romans, the great New Testament statement on justification, applies the teaching to actual Christian living in its last chapters. The book of Hebrews follows the same approach, presenting Jesus as our High

Priest in the heavenly sactuary and concluding with an explanation of how our faith in that High Priest is reflected in courageous, spiritual daily life.

Goldstein is well qualified both from experience and study to speak to these issues. He has lived and worked with those who have fallen off the path to one side or the other. As such, he has come to know the pitfalls of both sides, and he warns us against both. He has not found it easy to maintain balance, but through his own difficulties, Goldstein has developed a heart-felt message that he urges fellow Christians to heed. We do well to listen to his thoughtful insights.

William H. Shea
Biblical Research Institute
General Conference of Seventh-day Adventists
Silver Spring, Maryland

# Chapter 1

# Crow Eaters

**N**ever have Adventists had more reason to rejoice in, believe in, and trust in the three angels' messages and their fulfillment. Christ's words, "Lift up your heads; for your redemption draweth nigh" (Luke 21:28), burn with a pertinence unlike ever before. Only those with spiritual rigor mortis can fail to see how fast final scenes are unfolding. Events foretold in *The Great Controversy* are no longer for the future only. They are for now.

For years Adventists have asked, "How can the end-time scenario be fulfilled as long as the world faces a militant, well-armed Communism?" For some, the hammer and sickle (about which the prophetic pages are apparently silent) battered and sliced away at their confidence in the church's last-day message. Skeptics within the church questioned Ellen White for "picking on" Catholics, when every red-blooded, flag-waving Adventist American patriot could see that the enemy was not the pope, but the Communists. Now, however, Communism has gone belly up, and as the Catholic Church, feeding on its carcass, grows more powerful and influential every day—the skeptics eat crow.

"Catholicism," Ellen White wrote, "is gaining ground upon every side."[1] While these words haven't caught the details, they have identified the trends. The Catholic Church has been attaining power and influence not seen since the days when, with impunity, the "Holy Fathers" could burn their enemies at the stake. "Papal prestige today is very high," writes former Jesuit Peter De Rosa. "In this century, pontiffs have achieved world renown. Historic events and instant communication have contributed to make them 'Spokesmen of Religion.' "[2] John Paul II, the present "Spokesman of Religion," confidently declared during one of his trips to liberated Eastern Europe, "This world must be conquered."[3]

In the United States the Catholic Church has made such impressive political strides that one conservative Catholic paper has said that this is "the beginning of the Catholic era in American history."[4] More than a century ago, Ellen White warned that the Protestants were "opening the door for the papacy to regain in Protestant America the supremacy which she has lost in the Old World."[5] What would she say today?

Meanwhile, the New Christian Right "has become part of the political establishment."[6] Now firmly entrenched in the political system, it has become less visible than before—and the less visible, the more dangerous. Threatening the wrath of God on those who don't vote "the biblical" position on everything from Star Wars to aid for the Contras just doesn't cut it in twentieth-century America. Realizing this, the New Right is purposely taking a more tactful, low-key approach—particularly at local and state levels. "Newcomers and the more politically experienced conservative Christians alike are demanding real political influence," writes Rob Gurwitt. "And, unnoticed by most of the national news media, they are beginning to get it."[7]

Americans may no longer be able to count on the Supreme Court to protect their religious freedoms, as they once did. In "a radical departure" from previous rulings that guard the religious rights of minorities, the Supreme Court upheld, 6-3 (notice those numbers), the dismissal from employment of some Oregonian Indians who used peyote for a religious ceremony. Admitting that the new ruling "will place at a disadvantage those religious practices that are not widely engaged in," Justice Scalia said that "the unavoidable consequence of democratic government must be preferred to a system in which each conscience is law."[8] In other words, if your religious practices conflict with the needs of the majority, you should no longer expect the Supreme Court to be as likely to protect your rights.

Dissenting justices warned that this ruling results in "a wholesale overturning of settled law concerning the religion clauses of our constitution." Even Sandra Day O'Connor, who voted with the majority, nevertheless called Scalia's opinion "incompatible with the nation's fundamental commitment to religious liberty."[9]

Year by year, step by step, the pages of *The Great Controversy* and Relevation 13 play out before our eyes, giving significance to these political and religious events. God has poured out light upon His people that the world cannot comprehend; and as events unfold, we have more reason to love and live this truth than ever before.

Yet, today, Adventism is suffering a crisis. At a time when we should be proclaiming our message from rooftops, we're cowering in the basement instead. Many don't know why they are Adventists, what they believe, or why they believe it. Thousands don't pay tithe, don't go to church, and many, especially the young, are leaving. Our church services, which should be exciting, powerful, and spirit filled, are often so dull that to call them "lukewarm" would be a compliment. Adventism today is suffering an identity crisis, a theological crisis, and a spiritual crisis. The result? A series of crucial questions for the church. If we don't know who we are, why bring others within our ranks? If we don't know what we believe, why teach it to others? If we don't have spiritual power, who will be drawn to us? How can we expect to give the world a message if we aren't sure of the message itself? We talk about receiving the latter rain, but a snowstorm is more likely to fall in Mecca in June.

Many theories have arisen, both from the right and from the left, to explain our malaise. Television, working mothers, liberal theologians, material prosperity, celebration churches, legalism, Jesuits, male-only ordination, the schools—all these and more have been blamed. Yet Adventism is too big, too diverse, for anyone to be able to categorize, with precision, the cause of our spiritual lethargy.

Whatever the reasons, one thing is certain: If we don't repent, if we don't turn around, our sins will destroy us.

"The Lord has been revealed to us in ever-increasing light. Our privileges are far greater than were the privileges of God's ancient people. We have not only the great light committed to Israel, but we have the increased evidence of the great salvation brought to us through Christ."[10] If ancient Israel suffered so severely for its sins, what will happen to us? "Is not the guilt of God's professed people as much greater than was that of ancient Israel, as the light which we enjoy is greater than theirs?"[11]

Though never more confident of the truth of the three angels' messages, never have I feared more for the fate of the messengers. This truth is going to illuminate the world with its glory, even if we linger in darkness. Like Israel, we have been entrusted with the truth, yet at times I'm no more optimistic about Adventism than Jeremiah was about Jerusalem.

Though no simple answer exists, until we Adventists understand our message, we will not understand our identity, mission, or purpose. And the only way we can understand our message is to return to its foundation, for not until we know where we came from can we know where we are going. The essence, the foundation of Seventh-day Adventism, whether we like it or not, whether we accept it or not, is the sanctuary service.

"The subject of the sanctuary was the key which unlocked the mystery of the disappointment of 1844," wrote Ellen White. "It opened to view a complete system of truth, connected and harmonious, showing that God's hand had directed the great advent movement and revealing *present duty as it brought to light the position and work of His people.*[12]

Despite the importance Ellen White placed on the sanctuary, much confusion and distortion exist today on the topic, which is why we are adrift. Most Adventists don't know very much about the sanctuary, while those who do usually don't understand what it teaches, particularly in regard to the investigative judgment. Yet, according to Ellen White, the sanctuary "brought to light the position and work of [God's] people." No wonder, then, we don't know our position, our work, or our message. No wonder we are blown around by "every wind of doctrine" (Ephesians 4:14). No wonder there's a crisis of faith and identity within our ranks. How could it be otherwise, when the sanctuary, the basis of our existence, has been so distorted or even lost?

The major problem is that we have an unbalanced presentation of the sanctuary. The earthly sanctuary system had two major parts: the sacrifice of the animal (which always included ministry in the first apartment), and the Day of Atonement in the second apartment. Today, within Adventism, some want to look only at the sacrifice and first-apartment ministry; others want to focus on the ministration of the blood in the second apartment only. Yet either one, alone, presents an incomplete gospel; together, they give the full message of the ministry of Jesus Christ.

My wife, a lifelong Adventist, described to me how she was taught the investigative judgment, exemplifying what happens when we emphasize the ministry in the second apartment without balancing it with the preceding sacrifice. "I was taught," my wife said, "that the judgment is going on in heaven right now, and that our names may come up at any time. We can't know when that happens, but when it does, our names are blotted out of the book of life if we are not absolutely perfect. We are lost. We won't know it, and we may keep on struggling to be perfect, even though probation has closed for us and we have no hope."

Such teaching is not "good news," nor is it an accurate picture of what happens in the investigative judgment. Nevertheless, this is what many Adventists believe, and with such a theology, who can blame people for leaving the church?

Responding to this imbalance, some want to limit the sanctuary to the sacrifice and first apartment, ignoring the service in the Most Holy Place on the Day of Atonement. For them, the plan of salvation ends at the altar of burnt offering and the first apartment, with Jesus on the cross and forgiveness. The law, sanctification, judgment, victory over sin—all taught by the second apartment—become mere appendages of the "gospel." The fruit of such teaching can be seen in the adultery, divorce, substance abuse, stealing of tithe, and the general decline in standards and morality within the church. This false balance is not the only cause of such problems, of course, but it certainly has added to them.

Either imbalance, reducing the sanctuary to either the first apartment or the second, perverts the three angels' messages. By far, the latter teaching has become more prevalent in Adventism today, largely as a result of an earlier imbalance toward the former. To understand the sanctuary and what it says to the church today, we need the *whole* service—sacrifice in the first apartment and ministration in the second, each balanced with the other.

This book is a sequel to my *1844 Made Simple,* a study on deriving the date 1844 from the Bible, with a small section on the meaning of the investigative judgment. In this study, we will look at the sanctuary, particularly the investigative judgment, which, along with the sacrifice of Jesus, is the essence of the three angels' messages. We will study the biblical evidence for the investigative judgment and answer these questions:

Why does God have an investigative judgment?

Why does He even have a sanctuary in heaven? Is the sanctuary literal, and if so, why?

What happens when our name comes up in the judgment, especially in light of the cross?

What determines if our names remain or are blotted out of the book of life?

How do we balance the altar of burnt offering and the first apartment ministry, which symbolize the cross and justification, with the ministration of the blood in the Most Holy Place, which symbolizes the investigative judgment?

And finally, how do we reconcile Ellen White's statements about the character perfection of the final generation with justification by faith?

Prophecy is fulfilling before our eyes. Stupendous events unfold daily. Yet only a knowledge of, and an experience in, the complete sanctuary message can prepare us for what is coming.

---

1. *The Great Controversy,* p. 566.
2. Peter De Rosa, *Vicars of Christ: The Dark Side of the Papacy* (New York: Crown Publishers, 1988), p. 38.

3. *Washington Post* (April 23, 1990), p. A13.

4. *The Wanderer* (November 15, 1984).

5. *The Great Controversy,* p. 573.

6. Religious News Service (January 30, 1990), p. 4.

7. Rob Gurwitt, "The Christian Right Has Gained Political Power. Now What Does It Do With It?" *Governing* (October 1989), p. 52.

8. *The Fresno Bee* (April 18, 1990), p. 1-a.

9. Ibid.

10. *Christ's Object Lessons,* p. 317.

11. *Signs of the Times* (May 26, 1881).

12. *The Great Controversy,* p. 423. Emphasis supplied.

Chapter **2**

# Attack!

The subject of the sanctuary and the investigative judgment should be clearly understood by the people of God," wrote Ellen White. "All need a knowledge for themselves of the position and work of their great High Priest. Otherwise it will be impossible for them to exercise the faith which is essential at this time or to occupy the position which God designs them to fill."[1] Yet writing in *Christianity Today,* former Adventist David Neff has said that "few contemporary Adventists can explain it [the investigative judgment] and few Adventist theologians still teach it."[2]

If Neff is right, then most Adventists are obviously not where God wants them to be. Why?

The uniqueness of the sanctuary doctrine helps make it a prime target for attack. Though other major tenets of our faith—Sabbath, millennium, state of the dead—are accepted by other Christians, Adventists alone teach Christ's high priestly ministry in the second apartment, with its implications for an investigative judgment. This aspect of the sanctuary, "being uniquely our own, has also laid us open as a church to more opprobrium, ridicule, and scorn from other Christian churches than any other doctrine."[3]

The most insidious attacks, however, haven't come from other churches. After all, Adventists expect those who disagree with them on other doctrines to do the same regarding an investigative judgment. More dangerous are those who keep Sabbath, eat vege-links, and understand the state of the dead, yet who cast doubt on the idea of the sanctuary and on investigative judgment. By far, Satan's greatest assaults have come from within.

Dudley M. Canright (1840-1919), minister, church administrator, and writer, resigned his position in 1887, left Adventism, and became a Baptist preacher—all over the sanctuary doctrine. In his widely circulated book, *Seventh-day Adventism Renounced,* he claimed that the "Adventists' idea of the sanctuary in heaven is an absurdity."[4]

Albion Fox Ballenger (1861-1921), president of the Irish and Welsh missions, apostasized over the same teaching. He believed that prior to the cross, services were conducted in the first apartment of the heavenly sanctuary by angels who administered pardon under an immortal high priest named Melchizedek. The heavenly Day of Atonement, he taught, began at the cross, thus leaving no room for an investigative judgment beginning in 1844.

Louis Richard Conradi (1856-1939), president of the European Division until 1922, left the church over the sanctuary doctrine. An avid student of history, Conradi believed that the 2,300 days of Daniel 8:14 dealt only with Islam and that in 1844, God compelled the Mohammedans "to exercise tolerance toward all who would be Christians."[5]

In the past decade, Desmond Ford, speaker, theologian, and teacher, was defrocked for denying the investigative judgment. In a deeper, more intelligent review of some of Ballenger's ideas, Ford claimed that Christ entered the Most Holy Place in the heavenly sanctuary at His ascension. By using the apotelesmatic principle, which allows multiple interpretations of prophecy, Ford rejected the historical concept of the investigative judgment.

Though these men have been the most influential ones to challenge the sanctuary doctrine, others—often under their influence—have done so as well. And while some, such as Ford, had the courage to speak out, even at the cost of their paychecks, how many others, harboring and spreading similar doubts—remain within?

---

1. *The Great Controversy*, p. 488.
2. "A Santuary Movement," *Christianity Today* (February 5, 1990), p. 20.
3. Arnold V. Wallenkampf, "Challenges to the Doctrine of the Sanctuary," in *Doctrine of the Sanctuary*, ed. Frank Holbrook (Silver Spring, Md.: Biblical Research Institute, 1989), p. 198.
4. *Seventh-day Adventism Renounced*, 14th ed. (New York, 1889), p. 128.
5. Quoted in *Doctrine of the Sanctuary*, p. 207.

Chapter **3**

# The Missing Text

**W**hile some onslaughts against our sanctuary doctrine, particularly from within—such as the contention that Christ's blood would have dried up by 1844 and therefore couldn't be used in the heavenly sanctuary—are too frivolous to bother with, other questions have been honest and carefully thought out. Fortunately, the Lord has provided us with honest and carefully thought-out answers.[1]

One serious charge, circulated in recent years, claims that Adventists base the investigative judgment on Daniel 8:14 alone: "He said unto me, Unto two thousand and three hundred days; then shall the sanctuary be cleansed." "Good theology" does not establish a doctrine on a single text. None of our other distinctive teachings, such as the Sabbath or the state of the dead, rest on one verse only. What about the investigative judgment?

To answer this charge, we first need to define the investigative judgment and then see if it is indeed based on one verse only. Here's my definition.

The investigative judgment is a pre-advent (before the second coming) judgment that occurs in heaven, in which all of God's true followers will be favorably judged before the onlooking universe. In this judgment, all who have professed to serve Christ (and are therefore written in the book of life) have their lives come in review before God, who ultimately determines whether they have been robed in His righteousness. If they have been and are true followers of Christ, then their names are retained in the books of heaven, their sins are blotted out, and they will be granted entrance into the New Jerusalem. If, however, their profession has been only that, a profession, without the robe of Christ's righteousness, then their names will be blotted out of the books during this judgment, and they will be denied entrance into the New Jerusalem.

Some opponents of the investigative judgment have argued that believers who have accepted Jesus as their Saviour do not come into judgment. They cite John 5:22, 24. "Thy Father judgeth no man, but hath committed all judgment unto the Son. . . . He that heareth my word, and believeth on him that sent me, hath everlasting life, and shall not come into condemnation."

However, notice what Paul says in the book of Hebrews: "Again, The Lord shall judge his people" (Hebrews 10:30). Notice, whom does Paul say that God will judge? His people. Clearly, God's people will face a future judgment (this verse was written years after the cross).

Peter wrote, "Judgment must begin at the house of God: and if it first begin at us, what shall the end be of them that obey not the gospel of God"? (1 Peter 4:17). According to Peter, then, not only are believers ("the house of God") judged, but judgment *starts with them!* These are just two of many verses in the Bible teaching that believers must face judgment.[2]

Daniel 7 portrays a judgment scene:

> I beheld till the thrones were cast down, and the Ancient of days did sit, whose garment was white as snow, and the hair of his head like the pure wool: his throne was like the fiery flame, and his wheels as burning fire. A fiery stream issued and came forth from before him: thousand thousands ministered unto him, and ten thousand times ten thousand stood before him: the judgment was set, and the books were opened (verses 9, 10).

Where is this judgment happening? On earth? With fiery streams, the Ancient of Days, and burning wheels, it hardly sounds like it. Daniel depicts here a heavenly scene and, therefore, these "thousand thousands" and "ten thousand times ten thousand" must be angels, symbolized by the two gold cherubim in the second apartment of the sanctuary, where judgment occurred in the earthly model.

Who is involved in the court scene? The same chapter of Daniel, verse 22, describing this judgment, says: "Until the Ancient of Days came, and judgment was given to the saints of the most High; and the time came that the saints possessed the kingdom." Other versions read that judgment was given "in favor of saints," or "in behalf of the saints," or "for the saints."

Are believers involved? Obviously, otherwise, how could judgment be rendered in their favor? Imagine being in a courtroom, but only as a spectator. Books, records, documents, affidavits are examined in a case, and then the verdict is given. The judge looks up, points to you, and says that judgment is given "in *your* favor," or "in *your* behalf." What's going on? If you weren't on trial, no judgment would be rendered for or against you. Only those judged have a verdict pronounced on them, either for bad or for good.

"There is therefore now no condemnation for those who are in Christ Jesus" (Romans 8:1, RSV). The text doesn't say, "There is therefore now no *judgment* for those who are in Christ Jesus," but no condemnation. Romans 8:1 is one of the greatest investigative judgment texts in Scripture; it *implies* a judgment of Christians, because a person couldn't even be considered for condemnation if he weren't facing a judgment, and yet this verse announces the verdict for those who are "in Christ Jesus." That verdict is "no condemnation"! Obviously, this verdict, like the one in Daniel 7, is "in favor of the saints."

When does the judgment scene in Daniel 7 take place?

Verse 22 says that after the judgment, the "saints possessed the kingdom." When do the saints possess the kingdom? At the second coming (see verses 13, 14, 25, 26). This judgment—involving believers and a judgment in their behalf—occurs before the second coming of Jesus. Clearly, it is a pre-advent judgment.

Daniel 12:1 reads:

At that time shall Michael stand up, the great prince which standeth for the children of thy people: and there shall be a time of trouble, such as never was since there was a nation even to that same time: and at that time thy people shall be delivered, every one that shall be found written in the book.

Because this verse talks about "a time of trouble, such as never was," it must be dealing with the end of the world prior to the second coming of Jesus (or Michael, as He is called here). Who is delivered? "Every one *found* written in the *book.*" Doesn't this imply some type of looking or inquiry? Obviously this verse teaches an investigation in the heavenly ledgers before the second coming.

Linked with this verse is Revelation 21:27. "There shall in no wise enter into it [the holy city] any thing that defileth, neither whatsoever worketh abomination, or maketh a lie: but they which are written in the lamb's book of life." Jesus told the disciples to rejoice not because you cast out demons, but because "your names are written in heaven" (Luke 10:20).

According to Scripture, those whose names "are written in heaven" or whose names are "found written in the book" or who are in the "lamb's book of life" will be saved. Now, contrast these words with Revelation 3:5: "He that overcometh, the same shall be clothed in white raiment; and *I will not blot out his name out of the book of life,* but I will confess his name before my Father, and before his angels" (italics supplied). Notice the common elements this verse shares with the judgment scene in Daniel 7:

| Revelation 3:5 | Daniel 7 |
| --- | --- |
| "angels" | "thousand thousands" |
| "my Father" | "Ancient of days" |
| "Jesus" | "Son of man" |
| "book" | "books" |

Believers have their names written in a book in heaven, the book of life, and it is crucial that their names remain there, because only the names retained are granted entrance into the Holy City. Names can be blotted out, and if they are, the people will be too!

"Whosoever therefore shall confess me before men, him will I confess also before my Father which is in heaven. But whosoever shall deny me before men, him will I also deny before my Father . . . in heaven" (Matthew 10:32, 33).

"I say unto you, Whosoever shall confess me before men, him shall the Son of man also confess before the angels of God: but he that denieth me before men shall be denied before the angels of God" (Luke 12:8, 9).

Jesus will either confess your name before the Father (the "Ancient of days") and His angels ("thousand thousands"), or He will deny you. The Greek word for *deny* can be translated "disavow," "reject," "refuse." The Bible says that Jesus is our Advocate: "If any man sin, we have an advocate with the Father, Jesus Christ the righteous" (1 John 2:1). Imagine that while you are on trial, your own lawyer denies you before the judge! These verses warn about a day of reckoning when Jesus either denies you, and you are lost, or Jesus confesses you, and you are forever sealed. Certainly this is a time of judgment, one way or the other, for those who have professed Christ.

Acts 3:19, 20 also links judgment with the last days before Jesus returns. "Repent ye therefore, and be converted, that your sins may be blotted out, when the times of refreshing shall come from the presence of the Lord, and he shall send Jesus Christ." Look at the elements: repentance, conversion, blotting out of sins, refreshing from the Lord, and the second coming. The reference to Christ's return (verse 20), as in Daniel 12:1, sets the time frame for the last days.

The elements here are tightly linked. The first, repentance, is a gift from God, but, as with all His gifts, we have to accept it, in this case by confessing our sins and asking for pardon.

Repentance is a step toward the next element: conversion. "And be converted." You can be an Adventist, believe in and understand the investigative judgment, but if you are not converted, if you haven't, by the power of the Holy Spirit, made a conscious decision to surrender your life totally to Jesus, then you aren't converted—and without conversion, you are lost.

If lost, then the next element in the verse doesn't apply to you. "*Repent* ye therefore, and be *converted,* that your *sins may be blotted out.*" Revelation 3:5 infers that the names of those who aren't saved will be blotted out. In contrast, these verses in Acts talk about blotting out the *sins* (not the *names*) of those who are saved, those who have repented and are converted. Apparently, if your name is blotted out, you are lost; if your sins are blotted out, you are saved.

Acts 3:19 really reads, "Repent ye therefore, and be converted, that your sins may be blotted out, so that the times of refreshing shall come from the presence of the Lord." What is this time of refreshing? Commenting on Acts 3:19, Ellen White wrote, "The great work of the gospel is not to close with less manifestation of the power of God than marked its opening. The prophecies which were fulfilled in the outpouring of the former rain at the opening of the gospel are again to be fulfilled in the latter rain at its close. Here are 'the times of refreshing' to which the apostle Peter looked forward."[3]

What does Acts 3:19, 20 teach? That in the last days, linked with the latter rain, linked with the second coming of Jesus, the sins of those who have repented and been converted are blotted out. Peter's call to repentance and conversion, linked with the blotting out of sins, teaches that those whose sins are blotted out are saved. In contrast, Revelation 3:5, 21:27, and Daniel 12:1, taken together, teach that those whose names are blotted out are lost.

Other important verses dealing with the judgment are in the fourteenth chapter of Revelation, in the three angels' messages. The first angel's message reads:

I saw another angel fly in the midst of heaven,

having the everlasting gospel to preach unto them that dwell on the earth, and to every nation, and kindred, and tongue, and people, saying with a loud voice, Fear God, and give glory to him; for the hour of his judgment is come: and worship him that made heaven, and earth, and the sea, and the fountains of waters (Revelation 14:6, 7).

While this angel is preaching the "everlasting gospel," what does he cry? "Fear God and give glory to him; for *the hour of his judgment is come.*" For this angel, the judgment is part of the "everlasting gospel." This point is crucial because some in the church today want to limit the "gospel" to what Christ has accomplished for us on the earth alone, confining the plan of salvation to the altar of burnt offering. This first angel, however, does not stop at the altar but includes the whole sanctuary, especially the second apartment, because that is where the judgment, which he announces, takes place.

These verses also prove that the gospel is being preached while the judgment is going on, and the messages of the next two angels help establish its time frame.

There followed another angel, saying, Babylon is fallen, is fallen, that great city, because she made all nations drink of the wine of the wrath of her fornication. And the third angel followed them, saying with a loud voice, If any man worship the beast and his image, and receive his mark in his forehead, or in his hand, the same shall drink of the wine of the wrath of God (Revelation 14:8-10).

The three angels' messages occur in the context of the last days, for they deal with the mark of the beast, a controversy that immediately precedes the second coming of Jesus. Obviously, the judgment heralded by the first angel must take place before Jesus returns.

The parable of the wedding feast illustrates a judgment of those who have accepted the gospel invitation (see Matthew 22:1-14). In Jesus' parable, a king prepares a marriage for his son and then sends forth "his servants to call them that were bidden to the wedding" (verse 3). When those bidden refused the invitation, the servants called others instead: "So those servants went out into the highways, and gathered together all as many as they found, both bad and good: and the wedding was furnished with guests. And when the king came in to see the guests, he saw there a man which had not on a wedding garment" (verses 10, 11). After being confronted by the king, the speechless guest was "cast . . . into outer darkness" (verse 13).

Those who rejected the invitation didn't face the scrutiny of the king. "He that believeth not," warned Jesus, "is condemned already" (John 3:18). The king "came in to see" only those who accepted the invitation. In the same way, the investigative judgment is for the professed followers of Christ only. Why? Because not everyone who professes Jesus is covered by His righteousness, just as the guest was not covered with a wedding garment. "Not every one that saith unto me, Lord, Lord, shall enter into the kingdom of heaven; but he that doeth the will of my Father which is in heaven" (Matthew 7:21).

Who calls Jesus, "Lord, Lord," except those who claim to serve Him? Yet Jesus plainly says that not all those who make that claim will enter the kingdom of heaven. According to the parable, those who enter, both "the bad and the good," receive a wedding garment, which is Christ's righteousness. When the king saw the guests, only those with the robe were spared; the one without it was cast away. Clearly, this parable illustrates a judgment by the king on *those who accepted the invitation to the wedding feast.* The ones covered by his robe had nothing to fear.

We could consider other verses that have to do with the investigative judgment (we haven't touched Hebrews or Leviticus), but what have we seen so far?

God's people face judgment: "Again, The Lord shall judge his people" (Hebrews 10:30).

Judgment occurs in heaven before the second coming: "The judgment was set, and the books were opened" (Daniel 7:10).

The saints are involved in the judgment: "Judgment was made in favor of the saints" (Daniel 7:22, NKJV).

At some point, either our names are blotted out of the books of heaven ("I will not blot out his name out of the book of life," Revelation 3:5), or our sins will be blotted out (see Acts 3:19). This must be a work of judgment because the result of blotting out either our names or our sins determines whether or not we will live forever with Jesus.

Let's look again at the definition of the investigative judgment given earlier in this chapter to see if Scripture supports it.

The investigative judgment is a pre-advent judgment that occurs in heaven (see Daniel 7; Revelation 14:6) in which all of God's true followers will be favorably judged before the onlooking universe ("judgment was given in behalf of the saints"; "thousand thousands ministered unto him"; "there is therefore now no condemnation"; see Daniel 7:22; 10; Romans 8:1). In this judgment, all who have professed to serve the living God (and therefore are written in the book of life) have their lives come in review before God ("Again, The Lord shall judge his people" [Hebrews 10:30]), who ultimately determines whether or not they have been robed in Christ's righteousness (Matthew 22:1-14). If they have been and are true followers of Christ, then their names are retained in the books of heaven (see Daniel 12:1; Revelation 21:27) while their sins are blotted out ("that your sins may be blotted out" [Acts 3:19]), and they will be granted entrance into the New Jerusalem. If, however, their profession has been only that, a profession, without the robe of Christ's righteousness, then their names will be blotted out of the books during this judgment (see Revelation 3:5), and they will be denied entrance into the New Jerusalem.

The investigative judgment is scriptural, and it clearly is not based on merely a single text. In fact, what is the one text that we *haven't* used in this chapter?

Of course, Daniel 8:14. "Unto two thousand and three hundred days; then shall the sanctuary be cleansed."

---

1. For a detailed analysis of the major questions, see volumes 1-5 of the Daniel and Revelation Committee Series, published by the Biblical Research Institute of the General Conference of Seventh-day Adventists. For a simpler study, see *1844 Made Simple* by Clifford Goldstein (Boise, Idaho: Pacific Press, 1988).
2. For a more detailed study on this topic, see *1844 Made Simple,* pages 14-16.
3. *The Great Controversy,* pp. 611, 612.

Chapter **4**

# Mini-Judgments

$\mathbf{I}$s the investigative judgment—the idea that God judges His people from His temple—biblical? Can we find scriptural parallels to the investigative judgment that suggest this teaching is not unique but a basic theme of the Bible? Do we find God issuing judgments from His temple, in a manner similar to the Adventists' understanding of the investigative judgment?

These are important questions.

The Adventist concept of the pre-advent judgment has held that God's judgment on His people is currently being conducted in His heavenly sanctuary. In OT times, whether judgment came from the earthly tabernacle, the earthly temple, or the heavenly temple, it came from a sanctuary God actively used at that time. Thus God's past judgment activity from His sanctuary provides a background for, and a biblical link to, what Adventists have had to say about that type of activity by God in the present.[1]

What, then, can the Old Testament background tell us about the judgment?

In Numbers 16, Korah, Dathan, and Abiram—along with 250 "princes of the assembly, famous in the congregation, men of renown" (verse 2)—rebelled during the wilderness sojourn: "And they gathered themselves together against Moses and against Aaron, and said unto them, Ye take too much upon you, seeing all the congregation are holy, every one of them, and the Lord is among them: wherefore lift ye up yourselves above the congregation of the Lord?" (verse 3).

They were saying, "We are all holy; we are all righteous. God is among us!" These weren't unbelievers, nor did they outwardly reject God. According to their words, they wanted larger responsibilities in God's service. The issue, therefore, was among those who professed to serve the Lord.

How did Moses reply? "He spake unto Korah and unto all his company, saying, Even to morrow the Lord will shew *who are his, and who is holy*" (verse 5, emphasis supplied). God would separate the holy from the unholy, the wheat from the tares, in His church. The next day, "they took every man his censer, and put fire in them, and laid incense thereon, and stood in *the door of the tabernacle of the congregation* [sanctuary] with Moses and Aaron. And Korah gathered all the congregation against them unto the *door of the tabernacle of the congregation:* and the glory of the Lord appeared unto all the congregation" (verses 18, 19, emphasis supplied).

The Lord then separated Korah, Dathan, and Abiram from the rest of the camp, "and the earth opened her mouth, and swallowed them up, and their houses, and all the men that appertained unto Korah, and all their goods" (verse 32). If that's not judgment, what is?

From whom did this judgment come? It came from God, of course. But from *where*? God's presence was manifested in the sanctuary, which was why the Bible says that every one had gathered at "the door of the tabernacle of the congregation." It was at the sanctuary that God manifested Himself; it was there that He judged the people.

In the same chapter, after the destruction of the rebellious princes, the children of Israel murmured against Moses and Aaron, saying, "Ye have killed the people of the Lord" (verse 41). The next verses say: "And it came to pass, when the congregation was gathered against Moses and against Aaron, that they looked toward *the tabernacle of the congregation:* and, behold, the cloud covered it, and the glory of the Lord appeared. And Moses and Aaron came before *the tabernacle of the congregation.* And the Lord spake unto Moses, saying, Get you up from among this congregation, that I may consume them as in a moment" (verses 42-45, emphasis supplied).

Again, God judged His professed people from the sanctuary. The judgments came from the earthly sanctuary because God, at that time, had manifested His presence there.

What about today? According to the New Testament, the Lord is now in the sanctuary in heaven. "Of the things which we have spoken this is the sum: We have such an high priest, who is set on the right hand of the throne of the Majesty in the heavens, a minister of the sanctuary, and the true tabernacle, which the Lord pitched, and not man" (Hebrews 8:1, 2).

If God issued His judgments upon His people from the earthly sanctuary when His presence was manifested there, can He not do the same from the sanctuary in heaven today?

Other examples from the Old Testament prove that God issued judgments, both favorable and unfavorable, upon *His people* from the earthly sanctuary, which, according to the New Testament, stood as an "example and shadow" (Hebrews 8:5) of the one in heaven.

In Numbers 14, after the twelve spies brought back "an evil report of the land" (Numbers 13:32), the children of Israel rebelled against the Lord, declaring, "Would God that we had died in the land of Egypt! or would God that we had died in this wilderness" (Numbers 14:2). As they rebelled, threatening to return to Egypt, "the glory of the Lord appeared *in the tabernacle of the congregation* before all the children of Israel" (verse 10, italics supplied). When God threatened to destroy them, Moses interceded, and God spared them. He did, however, issue a judgment upon them from His sanctuary. "Surely they shall not see the land which I sware unto their fathers, neither shall any of them that provoked me see it" (verse 23). Again, judgment was pronounced from the sanctuary upon God's people.

When Miriam and Aaron spoke against Moses because "of the Ethiopian woman whom he had married" (Numbers 12:1) and questioned his leadership, "the Lord spake suddenly unto Moses, and unto Aaron, and unto Miriam, Come out ye three unto the tabernacle of the congregation" (verse 4). There, the Lord appeared to them "in the pillar of the cloud, and stood in the door of the tabernacle" (verse 5) where He then issued His judgment upon Miriam—another example of God judging His people from the sanctuary.

Clearly, from these examples, the Bible teaches that God judged His people from the earthly sanctuary, where He was manifested at that time.

Psalms, too, teaches the same. Psalm 9, for example, begins with praise to God for all His "marvellous works" (verse 1), including the defeat of His people's enemies, which is attributed to His righteous judgments: "But the Lord sits enthroned for ever, he has established his throne for judgment; and he judges the world with righteousness, he judges the peoples with equity" (verses 7, 8, RSV).

A passage in the midst of this psalm says, "Sing praises to the Lord, who dwells in Zion" (verse 11, RSV), thus implying that God issued these judgments from the earthly temple in Jerusalem.

Psalm 60 begins with lament about a past defeat at the hands of Israel's enemies but promises that future victory will come because "God has spoken in his sanctuary" (verse 6, RSV). Apparently, the psalmist saw God's judgments upon Israel's enemies coming as a result of what He pronounced upon them from His sanctuary.

In Psalm 73, the author laments the "prosperity of

the wicked" (verse 3), who "have more than heart could wish" (verse 7), yet who have "set their mouth against the heavens" (verse 9). He doesn't understand why they are prosperous in iniquity. He then says, "When I thought to know this, it was too painful for me; until I went into the sanctuary of God; then understood I their end" (verses 16, 17). He then describes the final judgment that will come upon the wicked, something that he understood only from the sanctuary. Whatever he saw there made him understand God's righteous judgments.

These verses taken from the Old Testament link the sanctuary with God's judgments. In the next chapter, we will see even more evidence that God issues judgments from His sanctuary.

---

1. William Shea, *Selected Studies on Prophetic Interpretation* (Washington, D.C.: Biblical Research Institute, General Conference of Seventh-day Adventists, 1982), p. 2.

# 5

# The Investigative Judgment of Judah

In addition to the examples given in the previous chapter, an important "mini-judgment" appears in the book of Ezekiel. William Shea of the Biblical Research Institute calls it "The Investigative Judgment of Judah."[1]

Ezekiel begins: "Now it came to pass in the thirtieth year, in the fourth month, in the fifth day of the month, as I was among the captives by the river of Chebar, that the heavens were opened, and I saw visions of God" (Ezekiel 1:1).

This date is July, 592 B.C., three-and-a-half years before the siege of Jerusalem by Babylonian King Nebuchadnezzar, which began in January, 588 B.C. The city fell two-and-a-half years after the siege began. So, from the beginning of Ezekiel's prophetic call in verse 1 (592 B.C.) until the final destruction of the city (586 B.C.), six years passed. God had originally established His people in the promised land 800 years earlier. Therefore, Ezekiel gave his messages at the extreme end of Judah's existence as a sovereign nation. This portion of Ezekiel's ministry was, as Shea writes, "God's last warning message to His people." The time context is important in understanding what follows.

"I looked, and, behold, a whirlwind came out of the north, a great cloud, and a fire infolding itself, and a brightness was about it, and out of the midst thereof as the colour of amber, out of the midst of the fire" (verse 4).

Ezekiel then says that in the middle of this whirlwind were "four living creatures" that had the "likeness of a man" (verse 5) and each "had four wings" (verse 6). He then describes wheels that are part of the vision: "When the living creatures went, the wheels went by them: and when the living creatures were lifted up from the earth, the wheels were lifted up. Withersoever the spirit was to go, they went, thither was their spirit to go; and the wheels were lifted up over against them: for the spirit of the living creature was in the wheels" (verses 19, 20).

What Ezekiel sees is not static, but moving. The whirlwind "came out of the north." The creatures had wings, symbolic of motion. Wheels, too, denote motion, and these wheels moved. And, finally, the whole apparition was in motion.

"And they went everyone straight forward: whither the spirit was to go, they went" (verse 12; see also verses 9,

17, 21, 24). Whatever the prophet sees here moves!
What does he see?

> When they went, I heard the noise of their wings,
> like the noise of great waters, as the voice of the
> Almighty, the voice of speech, as the noise of an
> host. . . . And above the firmament that was over
> their heads was the likeness of a throne . . . and
> upon the likeness of the throne was the likeness as
> the appearance of a man above upon it. . . . As the
> appearance of the bow that is in the cloud in the day
> of rain, so was the appearance of the brightness
> round about. This was the appearance of the like-
> ness of the glory of the Lord. And when I saw it, I
> fell upon my face (verses 24, 26, 28).

Ezekiel sees a vision of the "glory of the Lord" on His
throne. Revelation 4:2, 3 uses similar imagery in describing the glory of God in heaven. The important point,
again, is that God is in *motion;* the whole apparition is
going somewhere. "His [God's] movement is intentional
and directional," writes Shea. "He is the one who orders
the wheels and the living beings to follow the direction in
which they are to travel with the firmament and the
throne."[2]

Where is God going? According to verse 1, He came
out of the north. From Ezekiel's position on the River
Chebar, the Lord was moving south, either in the direction of the exiles in Babylon or toward Judah and
Jerusalem. Although the vision in chapter 1 doesn't
specify God's destination, "it is clear," writes Shea,
"from what follows in chapters 9-11 that God was trav-

eling southwest to His temple in Jerusalem. In later chapters God is depicted as taking leave of the temple after having taken up His residence there for a period of time. The principal point of the vision in the first chapter of Ezekiel is that God was in transit by means of His celestial chariot to the site of His earthly residence, His temple in Jerusalem."[3]

Immediately after the vision in chapter 1, the Lord gives Ezekiel the commission to "speak my words" to the "rebellious nation of Judah." The following chapters contain a series of stern indictments. In some cases, Ezekiel acted out the warnings: he lay on his side for 390 days (see Ezekiel 4:5); he ate barley cakes mixed with dung to symbolize how the children of Israel would "eat their defiled bread among the Gentiles, whither I will drive them" (4:13); he shaved his head, burning some hair, smiting others, and scattering the rest, symbolic of impending judgments (see chapter 5:1-6). All through these chapters, God warned of judgments on Judah because of apostasy and rebellion, culminating in the great abominations depicted in chapter 8.

In this chapter, Ezekiel is given another vision of the appearance of God, similar to that in the first chapter: "Behold, the glory of the God of Israel was there, according to the vision that I saw in the plain" (8:4). The Lord then reveals to Ezekiel the abominations in Judah: "Son of man, seest thou what they do? Even the great abominations that the house of Israel committeth here, that *I should go far off from my sanctuary?*" (verse 6, emphasis supplied).

Where is God's presence manifested? In the sanctuary, because He speaks to Ezekiel about being driven "far off" from it. The book began with God coming from the north, but He is now in the Jerusalem sanctuary. The following verses in Ezekiel 9 show that He manifested Himself there in order to judge His people:

> The Lord said unto him [a man with a writer's inkhorn], Go . . . through the midst of Jerusalem, and set a mark upon the foreheads of the men that sigh and cry for all the abominations that be done in the midst thereof. And to the others he said in mine hearing, Go ye after him through the city, and smite: let not your eye spare, neither have ye pity: Slay utterly old and young, both maids, and little children, and women: but come not near any man upon whom is the mark; and begin at my sanctuary. Then they began at the ancient men which were before the house (9:4-6).

Notice the two classes: the faithful, who receive a mark on their foreheads, and the unfaithful, who will be destroyed. This separation does not concern the heathen, but the professed servants of God. Indeed, this judgment began at the temple of the living God, "my sanctuary," and with the "ancient men which were before the house." This chapter teaches that God judges His people, dividing between the righteous and the wicked among them. This separation occurred shortly before the execution of the judgment because just a few years later, Nebuchadnezzar and his army, as God had warned, leveled Jerusalem.

The important point is that this distinction between the righteous and the wicked occurs *while God's presence is*

49

*specially manifested in the sanctuary.* The execution of the judgment resulted from the decisions that He made while there. God came to His earthly temple to do a special work of judgment, one that divided between the righteous and the wicked among His professed people, preparing the righteous for deliverance and the wicked for punishment.

The idea of God *moving* to His temple for judgment is found other places in the Bible too. The judgment scene of Daniel 7:13 reads: "I saw in the night visions, and, behold, one like the Son of man *came* with the clouds of heaven, and *came* to the Ancient of days, and they *brought* him near before him" (emphasis supplied). Talking about the same judgment, verse 22 reads: "The Ancient of days *came,* and *judgment* was given to the saints of the most High" (emphasis supplied). Malachi 3, describing the investigative judgment, also has Deity in motion before a work of judgment. "The Lord, whom ye seek, shall suddenly come to his temple. . . . And he shall sit as a refiner and purifier of silver: and he shall purify the sons of Levi. . . . And I will come near to you to judgment" (Malachi 3:1, 3, 5).

In Ezekiel, God not only comes to His temple for judgment, but He leaves it once the decisions have been made regarding His people. In chapter 10, Ezekiel again receives a vision of the "glory of the Lord," just as he had by the River Chebar. Here, too, he sees a "throne" (verse 1), "wheels" (verse 9), "the living creature" (verse 20). Now, however, God, instead of coming to the sanctuary, is leaving it. In verse 4, "the glory of the Lord went up from the cherub, and stood over the threshold of the house"; in verse 18, "the glory of the Lord departed from off the threshold of the house;" and finally, "the glory of the Lord went up from the midst of the city" (11:23). Once the division between the faithful from the unfaithful was complete, God left the earthly sanctuary. The judgment was over.

As the past two chapters have shown, numerous passages throughout the Old Testament picture God judging His people from His sanctuary. Is not this what the investigative judgment teaches—God, from His sanctuary (the heavenly one today) judging His people? We have seen, too, that in some instances the judgment involved a separation among those who have professed to serve the living God—between the faithful and the unfaithful. Is not the idea of separation between the wheat and the tares also part of Adventism's understanding of the investigative judgment?

These examples are "mini-judgments" that occurred in connection with localized events around and in the Middle East. The investigative judgment, however, as depicted in the books of Daniel and Revelation, is a world-wide judgment. The Lord, from His heavenly temple, will separate the faithful from the unfaithful among those, all over the world, who have professed to serve Him. "The OT judgment passages out of Daniel," writes Shea, "are a series of mini-judgments on the microcosmic scale, as it were. These lead up to, point to, and provide an earlier reflection of and a parallel to the great final judgment on the macrocosmic scale as described in Daniel (and the Revelation)."[4]

Yet important questions still need to be answered: Why does God have a judgment in heaven? If God knows everything, including "them that are his" (2 Timothy

2:19), then why the need for the judgment, and what does it mean for those of us who will one day have to stand in that judgment? In the following chapters, we will examine these questions.

1. See William Shea, *Selected Studies on Prophetic Interpretation* (Washington, D.C.: Biblical Research Institute, 1982), pp. 13-24.
2. Ibid., p. 15.
3. Ibid.
4. Ibid., p. 24.

Chapter **6**

# The Manifold Wisdom of God

Even after millennia, the aborted sacrifice of Isaac on Mount Moriah still burns into us its message of faith and obedience. Jews, Christians, and Muslims remain awed by this epic. The story endures, one of the most poignant in all Scripture.

After the command to offer Isaac as a burnt offering, Abraham bound him on the altar, and then, as he lifted the knife to slay the boy, an "angel of the Lord" cried out, "Lay not thine hand upon the lad, neither do thou any thing unto him: for now I know that thou fearest God" (Genesis 22:12).

The angel learned something about Abraham he didn't know before, which was that Abraham truly feared (respected) God. Had the angel reason to doubt? Though a man of faith, Abraham had at times shown a lack of trust in the Lord, such as when he lied to Pharaoh about his wife, or when he took Hagar to produce a child rather than believe God's promise that Sarah would be the "mother of nations; [that] kings of people shall be of her" (Genesis 17:16). After Abraham placed his son upon the altar and lifted the knife, however, there were no more questions regarding Abraham's trust and loyalty. Whatever doubts the angel might have harbored about Abraham's faith now vanished.

Did God put Abraham through such a severe trial merely to show an angel the patriarch's faith? Certainly the Lord knew Abraham's heart; He knew what would happen on that mountain. Was such a test really necessary—and if so, why?

Ellen White wrote:

> The sacrifice required of Abraham was not alone for his own good, nor solely for the benefit of succeeding generations; but it was also for the instruction of the sinless intelligences of heaven and of other worlds. The field of the controversy between Christ and Satan—the field on which the plan of redemption is wrought out—is the lesson book of the universe. Because Abraham had shown a lack of faith in God's promises, Satan had accused him before the angels and before God of having failed to comply with the conditions of the covenant, and as unworthy of its blessings. . . . Heavenly beings were witnesses of the scene as the faith of Abraham and

the submission of Isaac were tested. . . . All heaven beheld with wonder and admiration Abraham's unfaltering obedience. . . . Satan's accusations were shown to be false.[1]

These words introduce a crucial concept for a proper comprehension not only of the investigative judgment, but of the gospel itself. In Abraham's great test of faith, we see the interest of the universe in the plan of salvation. The cross, the sanctuary service, the judgment, the remnant, the law, character development—almost all our doctrines don't *quite* make sense unless we can see that the whole intelligent universe has a stake in the great controversy. The issues involving sin and Satan's accusations against God go far beyond the salvation of man, which is part of a bigger cosmic picture.

Where did the issue of sin and the great controversy originate? In the Garden of Eden, with Adam and Eve at the tree of the knowledge of good and evil? Is earth where sin began?

Of course not! The controversy began in another part of the universe, with the fall of Satan. "How art thou fallen from heaven, O Lucifer, son of the morning! how art though cut down to the ground, which didst weaken the nations!" (Isaiah 14:12). Sin, therefore, is not just a human problem. But though the rebellion began in another corner of the universe, it is fought on earth, where it will ultimately be resolved.

The book of Job is a microcosm of this great controversy between Christ and Satan.[2] The first scene, in heaven, reveals tension and conflict. Satan makes accusations against the Lord before the onlooking "sons of

God" (Job 1:6), apparently unfallen beings who are witnesses to the conflict. Is not this how the great controversy began: with Satan making accusations against God before the universe?[3]

The story of Job then shifts to the earth, where at first everything is idyllic, just as the earth was before sin entered. Quickly the battle moves here, with man (in this case, Job) in the center. The conflict began in another part of creation but is being resolved on earth—while unfallen beings watch from other worlds.

"Let us remember that individually we are working in full view of the heavenly universe."[4] "We are made a spectacle unto the world, and *to angels,* and to men" (1 Corinthians 4:9, emphasis supplied).

> The plan of redemption had a yet broader and deeper purpose than the salvation of man. It was not for this alone that Christ came to the earth; it was not merely that the inhabitants of this little world might regard the law of God as it should be regarded; *but it was to vindicate the character of God before the universe.*[5]

Here is a crucial concept of present truth. Satan disparaged God's character before the universe, bringing up questions about His government, law, and justice. Therefore, Christ came to earth to "vindicate the character of God before the universe."

Did the universe, therefore, have all its questions about God's character resolved by the life and death of Jesus? Were Satan's charges fully exposed by Christ, especially on Calvary? Here the angels and other sinless beings saw their beloved Commander—whom they had worshiped in the grandeur of heaven—now clothed in human flesh, beaten, scourged, mocked, and spat upon. Here they saw the One who had created the universe, the One whom they had praised in His celestial glory, brought to the dregs of human existence by His own hateful, ungrateful creatures. Here they saw the greatest example of selfless love ever manifested in the history of the eternity. Surely Christ's death on the cross should have sufficiently answered every charge!

All heaven and the unfallen worlds had been witnesses to the controversy. With what intense interest did they follow the closing scenes of the conflict.[6]

But was everything resolved for them?

Heaven viewed with grief and amazement Christ hanging upon the cross, blood flowing from His wounded temples, and sweat tinged with blood standing upon His brow. . . . All heaven was filled with wonder when the prayer of Christ was offered in the midst of His terrible suffering, "Father, forgive them; for they know not what they do." (Luke 23:24).[7]

But was everything resolved for them?

There stood men, formed in the image of God, joining to crush out the life of His only-begotten Son. What a sight for the heavenly universe![8]

But was everything resolved?

> Satan saw that his disguise was torn away. His administration was laid open before the unfallen angels and before the heavenly universe. He had revealed himself as a murderer. By shedding the blood of the Son of God, he had uprooted himself from the sympathies of the heavenly beings. . . . The last link of sympathy between Satan and the heavenly world was broken.[9]

But was everything resolved?

> Yet Satan was not then destroyed. The angels *did not even then understand all that was involved in the great controversy.* The principles at stake were to be more fully revealed. And for the sake of man, Satan's existence must be continued. Man as well as angels must see the contrast between the prince of light and the prince of darkness.[10]

In this connection, look at this verse of Scripture: "His intent was that now, through the church, the manifold wisdom of God should be made known to the rulers and authorities in the heavenly realms" (Ephesians 3:10, NIV).

Two important points leap out from this verse. First, by the time these words were written, about thirty years after Calvary, not all the "manifold wisdom of God" had been made "known to the rulers and authorities in the heavenly realms." In other words, even after the cross, the universe still needed to learn more about "the manifold wisdom of God."

But the most incredible idea brought out in this verse is *how* this wisdom will be made manifest. It says, "through the church." That is, through us, through all the faithful, "the manifold wisdom of God" will be revealed to the universe! As inconceivable as that concept sounds—it is what the Bible says.

Such a further manifestation of God doesn't take away the cross. It doesn't take away one iota from the truth that the full, complete penalty was paid by Jesus in our behalf at the cross so that every sinner, no matter his sin, can be accepted and fully pardoned. And it certainly doesn't take away from the incomprehensible love manifested at the cross. Instead, it proves that as far as the whole universe is involved (and they are involved), all their questions regarding the great controversy were not fully resolved at Calvary. And, as hard as it might be to believe, God is going to use His church, His people, to help resolve them.

"The church," Ellen White wrote, "is the repository of the riches of the grace of Christ; and through the church will eventually be made manifest, even to the 'principalities and powers in heavenly places,' the final and full display of the love of God."[11] Heavy thought. Yet failure to grasp this idea means failing to grasp an essential aspect of present truth.

A segment of Adventism dislikes the idea of our involvement in helping to resolve the great controversy. Instead, they preach "the cross, the cross, all done at the cross." Who can argue with cross-centered preaching? And while it might sound good, they preach a false Christ, an unbalanced gospel. A person can expound on the cross, have one tattooed on his arm, even carry a fifty-pound wooden one on his back, but he can at the same time twist what happened on the cross to the point that he makes a mockery of it.

Can a person attribute too much to the cross? Never, in terms of the love God manifested there. A billion years from now we will marvel at that love, still trying to comprehend the selflessness and mercy that went all the way to Calvary for us. Rather, can a person attribute too much to what was accomplished there?

What about those who teach "once saved always saved"? They believe that Christ's death on the cross was so efficacious, so complete, that if a person accepts what happened there, then he or she is eternally secure. That person, because of the cross, will be saved, no matter how far he disintegrates into sin. Because of what Jesus did at Calvary, this backslider is covered and will be taken into the presence of sinless beings for eternity.

Does not such a doctrine attribute too much to the cross in terms of what was accomplished there? Does it not actually pervert what happened there? Of course! Calvary, as complete as it is, makes no provision for those who, once saved by it, turn away, refusing to repent, refusing to confess, refusing to obey.

> For it is impossible for those who were once enlightened, and have tasted of the heavenly gift, and have become partakers of the Holy Spirit, and have tasted the good word of God and the powers of the age to come, if they fall away, to renew them again unto repentance; since they crucify again for themselves the Son of God, and put Him to an open shame (Hebrews 6:4-6, NKJV).

How about the universalists, those who teach that Christ's death on the cross was so complete that every human being—from Genghis Kahn to Hitler—will be saved? Aren't they, too, attributing too much to the cross, again in terms of what was accomplished there? Of course. Though Calvary provided salvation for the whole world, it wasn't so complete that it automatically saved the whole world. People will be lost. " 'For behold, the day is coming, burning like an oven, and all the proud, yes, all who do wickedly will be stubble. And the day which is coming shall burn them up,' says the Lord of hosts, 'that will leave them neither root nor branch' " (Malachi 4:1, NKJV).

Too much can be attributed to what was accomplished at the cross, also, in terms of the plan of salvation as it relates to the great controversy. Obviously, the battle with Satan didn't end at the cross because he still prowls the planet, devouring and deceiving mankind. Men continue to sin. God's law is still trampled upon; and the earth still shudders from evil. If *everything* was accomplished at Calvary, why are we still here 2,000 years later?

As the next chapter shows, the cross didn't end the plan of salvation—it began it!

---

1. *Patriarchs and Prophets*, pp. 154, 155.
2. See Clifford Goldstein, *How Dare You Judge Us, God!* (Boise, Idaho: Pacific Press, 1991).
3. See *Patriarchs and Prophets*, pp. 33-42.
4. *Testimonies for the Church*, vol. 8, p. 164.

5. *Patriarchs and Prophets,* p. 68, emphasis supplied.
6. *The Desire of Ages,* p. 759.
7. Ibid., p. 760.
8. Ibid.
9. Ibid., p. 761.
10. Ibid., emphasis supplied.
11. *The Acts of the Apostles,* p. 9.

Chapter **7**

# The Manifold Wisdom of God (Cont.)

The Jewish sanctuary service, whether in the wilderness or in Jerusalem, was composed of the sacrifice of the animal and the ministration of the shed blood. All Christians agree that the death of an innocent animal, which died instead of the sinner, symbolized the death of Jesus, who died for the sins of the world. All the lambs, the goats, the bullocks, and the pigeons were symbols of Christ, who "died for the ungodly" (Romans 5:6).

In every service that called for blood, the animal sacrifice *began* the temple procedure. The service didn't end with the animal being slain on the altar; it *started* there. Depending on the sin or who sinned, an elaborate temple ritual took place *after* the sacrifice, just as Christ's high priestly ministry in the heavenly sanctuary took place after His death on Calvary.

The Bible makes it clear that though one aspect of Christ's work was indeed finished at the cross—Jesus Himself crying, "It is finished!" (John 19:30)—He is still involved in a work of salvation. The book of Hebrews repeats again and again that Christ is now ministering in the sanctuary in heaven, exactly in the same order that the ministration in the earthly sanctuary took place: sacrifice first (Calvary), and then temple ministration (the sanctuary in heaven).

"The forerunner has entered [the heavenly sanctuary] for us, even Jesus, having become High Priest forever according to the order of Melchizedek" (Hebrews 6:20, NKJV).

"Therefore He is also able to save to the uttermost those who come to God through Him, since He ever lives to make intercession for them" (Hebrews 7:25, NKJV).

"This is the main point of the things we are saying: We have such a High Priest, who is seated at the right hand of the throne of the Majesty in the heavens, a Minister . . . of the true tabernacle which the Lord erected, and not man" (Hebrews 8:1, 2, NKJV).

"Christ came as High Priest of the good things to come, with the greater and more perfect tabernacle not made with hands, that is, not of this creation" (Hebrews 9:11, NKJV).

"Christ has not entered the holy places made with hands, which are copies of the true, but into heaven itself, now to appear in the presence of God for us" (Hebrews 9:24, NKJV).

What do these verses about Christ's ministration in the heavenly sanctuary mean if everything was finished at the cross? What is Jesus doing there? Cooling His heels? Wasting time? Obviously, He is doing something in the heavenly sanctuary as a High Priest that He didn't accomplish on earth as a lamb. In the same way, the priest in the earthly temple had a different function than did the sacrificial animal. Jesus, however, served in both roles. He was first the sacrificial animal—"Behold the Lamb of God, which taketh away the sin of the world" (John 1:29)—and *then* the High Priest in the sanctuary in heaven.

Christians who don't understand Christ's high priestly ministry can't fully understand the cross, anymore than a Jew in ancient Israel could understand the full significance of the animal sacrifice without understanding what happened to that shed blood when brought to the sanctuary. The plan of salvation consists of the cross *and* the ministration in the heavenly sanctuary. Without a proper comprehension of both, neither makes complete sense.

Not everything was totally resolved at the cross because everything was not finished there, as Ephesians 3:10, 11 reveals: "His intent was that now, through the church, the manifold wisdom of God should be made known to the rulers and authorities in the heavenly realms, *according to his eternal purpose which he accomplished in Christ Jesus our Lord*" (Ephesians 3:10, 11, NIV, emphasis supplied).

According to these verses, not only is the Lord planning to use the church, through Jesus, to reveal His wisdom to the universe, but this plan is part of "God's eternal purpose." We often think of Christ's death as planned from the beginning—"the Lamb slain from the foundation of the world" (Revelation 13:8)—and it was! But these verses say that according to God's "eternal purpose," we—the church, His true people, wherever, whoever they are—have a role that was planned from the beginning too.

But how is "the church" to be used? How can we be used to "make known to the rulers and authorities in the heavenly realms" the manifold wisdom of God as He has "purposed in Christ Jesus our Lord"?

Ephesians 2:10 reads: "We are His workmanship, created in Christ Jesus for good works, which God prepared beforehand that we should walk in them" (NKJV). This verse proves that not only were we created "for good works" but that these works were "prepared beforehand" or (as the KJV says) "before ordained." Just as God planned from the beginning to use the church to reveal His wisdom to the universe, so He also planned as part of His eternal purpose that we should do "good works." Is there any connection between these two ideas?

God says, "I have created him [those called by His name] for my glory, I have formed him; yea, I have made him" (Isaiah 43:7).

"Above all lower orders of being," Ellen White writes, "God designed that man, the crowning work of His creation, should express His thought and reveal His glory."[1]

Apparently, then, we were created for two basic purposes: for good works, and for the glory of God. Could there be a connection between the two?

"Let your light so shine before men, that they may see your good works, and glorify your Father which is in heaven" (Matthew 5:16).

According to Jesus, God is glorified by our good works. "Herein is my Father glorified," He said, "that ye bear much fruit" (John 15:8). God is glorified by the deeds, works, and the character development of His people. "The honor of God," Ellen White writes, "the honor of Christ, is involved in the perfection of the character of His people."[2]

Of course, the character of God's people is not the only factor affecting the honor of God. The cross of Christ is no doubt the major demonstration vindicating God's character, but it is not the only one. Obviously, God has decided that in addition to what happened at the cross He is going to use His people to honor Him before the universe.

"It becomes every child of God," writes Ellen White, "to vindicate His [God's] character."[3]

The idea of God being glorified in His people, by their deeds, actions, and character, is nothing new. It was a prime reason that God called out Israel to be a special people unto Himself. He had wanted an entire nation to reflect His character to the world and thus bring Him glory.

"[He] said unto me, Thou art my servant, O Israel, in whom I will be glorified" (Isaiah 49:3).

"Sing, O ye heavens; for the Lord hath done it: shout, ye lower parts of the earth: break forth into singing, ye mountains, O forest, and every tree therein: for the Lord hath redeemed Jacob, and glorified himself in Israel" (Isaiah 44:23).

"Thy people also shall be all righteous: they shall inherit the land for ever, the branch of my planting, that I may be glorified" (Isaiah 60:21).

"To appoint unto them that mourn in Zion, to give unto them beauty for ashes, the oil of joy for mourning, the garment of praise for the spirit of heaviness; that they might be called trees of righteousness, the planting of the Lord, that he might be glorified" (Isaiah 61:3).

"I do not this for your sakes, O house of Israel, but for mine holy name's sake, which ye have profaned among the heathen" (Ezekiel 36:22).

The issues of sin, evil, and salvation are so much bigger than us. Though humankind's redemption through the cross of Christ forms the focus and center of the gospel, the plan of salvation itself involves questions that extend far beyond merely getting our bodies off the dying planet. The real concern deals with the character of God Himself. Is He fair? Is He just? Does He deserve the worship, loyalty, and adoration of His creation?

A few years ago, I studied the book of Daniel with a Jewish friend. Though impressed by the prophecies, he said: "OK, this is all very interesting, and maybe there really is a God out there. But even if there is, when I look at the world—the pain, the heartache, the injustice—I think that, even if God exists, why should I worship Him? Very little of what I see makes me think that He is worthy of worship and praise."

"You don't realize," I responded, "just how fundamental that question is. You are asking the paramount question of the whole universe, a question that was first asked even before the creation of the world."

Was not this the question Lucifer asked in heaven? And here, thousands of years later, in a small apartment in Takoma Park, Maryland, this man, knowing nothing of the great controversy that began in a corner of the creation ages ago, repeated in a different form the same question that started the whole rebellion.

This question about God's character has continued through the ages and remains still today. So the Lord will ultimately answer these questions regarding His justice and fairness to the satisfaction of all creation.

> He that ruleth in the heavens is the one who sees the end from the beginning—the one before whom the mysteries of the past and future are alike outspread, and who, beyond the woe and darkness and ruin that sin has wrought, beholds the accomplishments of His own purposes of love and blessing. Though "clouds and darkness are round about Him: righteousness and judgment are the foundation of His throne." Psalm 97:2, R.V. And this the inhabitants of the universe, both loyal and disloyal, will one day understand. "His work is perfect: for all His ways are judgment: a God of truth and without iniquity, just and right is He." Deuteronomy 32:4.[4]

As hard as it is to believe, the Lord wants to use His people to help answer these questions. Our characters are, as Ellen White said, "involved" in bringing honor to God. They are not everything; other factors play a role in the issues, but we are still part of the plan. By far, the life and death of Jesus is the center. The cross, and what Jesus has accomplished for us there, is like the hub of a wheel. It forms the nucleus, the core, and all other truth, like the spokes, emanates from this central point. As in a wheel, however, the spokes have an important part to play.

Of course, anything that we can do to honor and glorify the Lord comes only because of what Jesus has done and is doing for us and in us. And all that He does for us comes only because of the cross.

"Work out your own salvation with fear and trembling. For it is God which worketh in you both to will and to do of his good pleasure" (Philippians 2:12, 13).

"Christ in you, the hope of glory" (Colossians 1:27).

"Without me," Jesus said, "ye can do nothing" (John 15:5).

Only by coming to the cross broken in spirit and confessing our sins, relying wholly on His merit worked out for us and in behalf of us at Calvary, can we be used by God. Without a born-again experience, we can no more give glory to the Lord than a lobster can do the polka. Only by responding to the call of the Holy Spirit, then yielding ourselves unreservedly to the power of God, and then fighting the fight of faith in His power by daily choosing to surrender ourselves to His purifying and refining power, can we become the kind of people that He is seeking for Himself, a people whose lives will give honor and glory to His name.

This concept helps form the meaning of the three angels' messages of Revelation 14. "I saw another angel fly in the midst of heaven, having the everlasting gospel . . . saying with a loud voice, Fear God, and give glory to him; for the hour of his judgment is come" (Revelation 14:6, 7). These messages share "the everlasting gospel," which has its foundation, its essence, its being in Christ on the cross. Then the messages continue by saying to give "glory to God." The only way we can do that is to have a born-again experience, which comes only when one is saved. Salvation results in obedience, which is why the third angel's message says, "Here is the patience of the saints: here are they that keep the commandments of God, and the faith of Jesus" (Revelation 14:12). Is there a connection between the everlasting gospel, having the faith of Jesus, keeping the commandments, and giving glory to the Lord? Of course. All are inseparable.

Also, in the three angels' messages is the phrase, "the hour of his judgment is come." The next chapters reveal how judgment, the cross, and the character of God's people are all linked into an inseparable chain of present truth.

---

1. *Testimonies for the Church,* vol. 8. p. 264.
2. *The Desire of Ages,* p. 671.
3. *Testimonies for the Church,* vol. 5, p. 312.
4. *Patriarchs and Prophets,* p. 43.

# Chapter 8

# Israel's Sanctuary

**D**espite the amazing condescension of the Son of God in dying for our sins, questions remained for the "principalities and powers in heavenly places" regarding "the manifold wisdom of God" even after Calvary. As we saw in the last chapter, the Lord intends to use His people to help resolve the issues for the onlooking universe. "The honor of God, the honor of Christ," Ellen White writes, "is involved in the perfection of the character of His people."[1]

Will anything else, besides the cross and the character of God's people, be involved in answering these questions? The answer is yes. And here, too, as the next few chapters will show, the key is in the earthly sanctuary service.

"Unto us was the gospel preached, as well as unto them [ancient Israel]: but the word preached did not profit them, not being mixed with faith in them that heard it" (Hebrews 4:2).

The gospel was preached to ancient Israel through the sanctuary service, a pictorial representation of the entire plan of salvation. How much the Jews understood of God's plan, we don't know, but enough must have been revealed to make it possible to be saved by the gospel message taught through the temple service. The sanctuary, in shadows, revealed atonement, mediation, priesthood, confession, cleansing, the law, the blotting out of sin, forgiveness, sanctification, justification, and the role of Satan (the scapegoat).

From the wanderings of the children of Israel in the wilderness to the destruction of the temple by the Romans in A.D. 70, the sanctuary service—with a few exceptions (such as the Babylonian captivity)—stood as the center of Israelite worship. Their entire religious system revolved around the sanctuary, just as Christianity revolves around Jesus Christ.

All who did service in connection with the sanctuary were being educated constantly in regard to the intervention of Christ in behalf of the human race. This service was designed to create in every heart a love for the law of God, which is the law of His kingdom. The sacrificial offering was to be an object lesson of the love of God revealed in Christ—in the suffering, dying victim, who took upon Himself the sin of which man was guilty, the innocent being made sin for us.[2]

Israel, over the centuries, built four sanctuaries, or temples: the Mosaic sanctuary, Solomon's temple, Zerubbabel's temple, and Herod's temple. So dominant has the temple been to Judaism that some Jews hope that another temple will be constructed in Jerusalem at the site of the old ones (where one of the holiest shrines in Islam, the Dome of the Rock, now sits). Some have even been training in a fourteen-year course on how to offer animal sacrifices as well as minister in a rebuilt temple. In the early 1980s, Israeli authorities arrested some Jews for trying to blow up the Dome of the Rock in order to pave the way for the temple. Apparently, even after 1,900 years, the temple looms large in the psyche of ultra-orthodox Judaism.

Though the different temples varied in size (the two apartments in Solomon's temple were twice as large as in the Mosaic one), their function and ritual followed the basic pattern disclosed to Moses on Mount Sinai. The wilderness sanctuary was the foundation for the later temples. For example, the New Testament book of Hebrews doesn't view Solomon's temple, the biggest, most elaborate of Israel's sanctuaries, as the quintessence of the Hebrew faith. And though many aspects of the Jewish religion matured over the centuries, the worship conducted in Herod's temple, the last temple, was not the apogee of Judaism's evolutionary development. On the contrary, the book of Hebrews focuses on Israel's first sanctuary, the wilderness tabernacle, as the earthly example of "the true tabernacle" in heaven. The wilderness tabernacle served as "the copy and shadow of the heavenly things" (Hebrews 8:5, NKJV).

In the Bible, most of the information given about the

sanctuary deals with the first one, the Mosaic structure built in the wilderness. One-third of the book of Exodus deals with the organization and construction of that first sanctuary; most of Leviticus deals with its rituals. If anything, the later temples, which didn't contain the ark of the covenant found in the wilderness structure, served only as elaborate copies of the Sinai prototype.

Unfortunately, the Old Testament itself, while giving massive details concerning the construction of the earthly sanctuary as well as the sacrificial rituals, does not clearly explain their meaning. Nor do the prophets, in most cases, decipher the symbolism. Fortunately, enough information has been revealed, particularly from the New Testament, that a basic understanding is clear.

The first part of the sanctuary service dealt with the sacrifice of the animal at the altar of burnt offering. Here is where the sanctuary service began. These sacrifices symbolized Jesus, who died once and for all at Calvary. He "does not need daily, as those high priests, to offer up sacrifices, first for His own sins and then for the people's, for this He did once for all when He offered up Himself" (Hebrews 7:27, NKJV).

"So Christ was offered once to bear the sins of many" (Hebrews 9:28, NKJV).

We have been sanctified through the offering of the body of Jesus Christ once for all. And every priest stands ministering daily and offering repeatedly the same sacrifices, which can never take away sins. But this Man, after He had offered one sacrifice for sins forever, sat down at the right hand of

God. . . . For by one offering He has perfected forever those who are being sanctified (Hebrews 10:10-
12, 14, NKJV).

Day after day, year after year, century after century,
these endless animal offerings pointed to Christ's death
at Calvary, the only efficacious sacrifice for sin. "For it is
not possible that the blood of bulls and goats could take
away sins" (Hebrews 10:4). The sacrificial system
pointed the worshiper *forward* to the cross; today, the
Christian, with his Bible, is pointed *back* to it.

How much the Israelite understood from the sacrificial system about salvation is not known. Moses explained in the wilderness that " 'the life of the flesh is
in the blood, and I have given it to you upon the altar
to make atonement for your souls; for it is the blood
that makes atonement for the soul' " (Leviticus 17:11).
The sinner probably saw that the "wages of sin is
death," and that God had provided a substitute to die
in the sinner's place.[3]

In the courtyard, between the altar of burnt offering
and the sanctuary structure itself, was a bronze laver
used by the priests for washing (see Exodus 30:17-19).
The Bible explains that the ministering priests were to
wash with the water in the laver, "lest they die" (verses
20, 21). Though not much else is said about the laver and
its meaning (see Exodus 38:8), apparently it somehow
signified cleansing and holiness, impressing upon the
people and the priest that "all defilement must be put
away from those who would approach into the presence
of God."[4]

The sanctuary building was basically an elaborate tent

made of fabrics and animal skins so that it could easily be taken apart and transported during the wilderness wanderings.[5] It consisted of two apartments, the Holy Place and the Most Holy Place. From within this structure, God manifested His presence to Israel. He said to the Israelites not long after the Ten Commandments were given at Sinai: "Let them make me a sanctuary; that I may dwell among them" (Exodus 25:8).

Within the first apartment, the Holy Place, stood the golden altar of incense, where every morning and evening the priest burnt "fragrant incense" to the Lord. Though the Bible doesn't explicitly explain its meaning, Solomon said to the Phoenician king Hiram, "Behold, I am about to build a house for the name of the Lord my God and dedicate it to him for the burning of incense of sweet spices before him" (2 Chronicles 2:4, RSV). Numerous times Scripture says that Israel sinned against the Lord by [burning] incense to other gods, "that they might provoke me to anger" (2 Chronicles 34:25, RSV). Apparently, burning incense on the altar in the Israelite sanctuary symbolized worship and adoration of the Deity. Luke 1:10 links it with prayer, which is also worship and adoration of God (see also Revelation 5:8; 8:3, 4).

In that same first apartment was a golden table on which was placed bread, incense, and wine, though only the bread is discussed in detail (see Leviticus 24:5-7). Possibly the bread symbolized an acknowledgment that God supplied not only salvation, but Israel's daily physical requirements. Some have seen a relationship between the bread and Jesus, who called Himself the "bread of life" (John 6:48).

The last piece of furniture in the first apartment was the seven-branched candlestick, the menorah, which was kept constantly burning. Besides providing light for the ministering priest, the lamp has been viewed as symbolic of the Holy Spirit. In a representation of the heavenly sanctuary shown to John the Revelator, he saw "seven golden lampstands, and in the midst of the seven lampstands One like the Son of Man, clothed with a garment down to the feet and girded about the chest with a golden band" (Revelation 1:12, 13, NKJV). The seven lamps could be analogous to the seven-branched candlestick of the first apartment, and the context of Revelation 1:4, 5 indicates that it is referring to the "seven Spirits who are before His throne" (NKJV), a reference, surely, to the Holy Spirit.

The first apartment service was a daily, continuous affair, symbolizing the constant availability of salvation and Christ's unceasing priestly ministry in our behalf. Here Israel obtained forgiveness, reconciliation, and restoration, in the same way that a sinner today, by coming to Jesus, obtains the same. In ancient Israel, a penitent sinner would bring his animal to the entrance of the sanctuary, it would be slain, and then the priest would apply the blood (the exact ritual depended on who the sinner was and what he had done).

Often, the priest brought the blood into the first apartment, while the sinner walked away, his sins forgiven— the same way that we, coming to Jesus by faith, have our sins forgiven as well.

In the sanctuary ritual, atonement was not made when the animal died. Only *after* the priest had mediated in behalf of the sinner by sprinkling the spilled blood in the appropriate place was atonement made. The priest shall take of the blood of the sin offering with his finger, and put it upon the horns of the altar of burnt offering and . . . the priest shall burn [the fat] upon the altar . . . *and the priest shall make an atonement for his sin that he hath committed, and it shall be forgiven him"* (Leviticus 4:34, 35, emphasis supplied). This formula is repeated over and over in the book of Leviticus, with atonement being made only *after* the blood was ministered by the priest.[6]

Adventists have been accused of not believing in a complete atonement (which, supposedly, is why we keep Sabbath, to work our way into heaven). If atonement (at-one-ment, or the bringing together of two estranged parties, such as man and God) means that the full, complete penalty for sin was paid at Calvary, that reconciliation was effected between man and God, and that nothing else can add or take away from the sacrifice—then, yes, definitely, atonement was completed at the cross. In the sanctuary service, after the sinner had slain the animal, all he could do was accept the sacrifice by faith (and all that faith entails).

If, however, atonement means that the final resolution of the sin problem has been settled at the cross, as well as the reestablishment of complete harmony throughout creation, with all the issues in the great controversy solved—then, no, obviously, atonement was not completed at Calvary.

In the earthly tabernacle service, the shed blood itself didn't make an atonement; it had to be brought into the sanctuary by the priest. Shed blood always had to be mediated; otherwise, it had no meaning. If the earthly system is merely a "shadow" of the heavenly, it's no wonder the Bible clearly depicts Jesus ministering in the heavenly sanctuary in our behalf in the same sense that the earthly priest ministered in behalf of the sinner in the old system. "He is also able to save to the uttermost those who come to God through Him, since He ever lives to make intercession for them" (Hebrews 7:25, NKJV).

If *everything* was finished at the cross, then why does this verse (and others) depict Jesus as a High Priest, making "intercession" in the heavenly sanctuary in behalf of His people? The answer, of course, is that not everything in terms of dealing with the sin problem was finished there.

Ellen White writes: "The intercession of Christ in man's behalf . . . is as essential to the plan of salvation as was His death upon the cross. By His death He began that work which after His resurrection He ascended to complete in heaven."[7] She says also that "the sanctuary in heaven is the very center of Christ's work in behalf of men. It concerns every soul living upon the earth. It opens to view the plan of redemption, bringing us down to the very close of time and revealing the triumphant issue of the contest between righteousness and sin."[8]

Rituals conducted in the first apartment, the Holy Place, were daily occurrences; the ritual that involved the second apartment, the Most Holy Place, occurred only once a year in the solemn ceremony of Yom Kippur, the Day of Atonement, or literally, "the day of covering."

What does that second-apartment ritual teach?

---

1. *The Desire of Ages,* p. 671.
2. *Selected Messages,* bk. 1, p. 233.

3. For a more detailed study, see *The Sanctuary and the Atonement,* published by the Biblical Research Committee of the General Conference of Seventh-day Adventists (Washington, D.C., 1981).

4. *Patriarchs and Prophets,* p. 350.

5. For more details on the construction itself, see Exodus 25-40.

6. See Leviticus 4:13-20; 4:22-26; 5:8-11. In all these examples and others, it is always the priest who makes the atonement, not the animal itself.

7. *The Great Controversy,* p. 489.

8. Ibid., p. 488.

# Chapter 9

# The Two Cherubim

In the second apartment of the wilderness sanctuary sat the most important object in the entire structure: the ark of the covenant. Standing alone in the Most Holy Place, this wooden box covered with gold contained Aaron's rod that budded, a pot of manna, and the two tablets on which were inscribed the Ten Commandments. Above the ark, on the gold lid known as the "mercy seat," were two gold angels with their wings spread:

> You shall make two cherubim of gold; of hammered work you shall make them at the two ends of the mercy seat. Make one cherub at one end, and

the other cherub at the other end; you shall make the cherubim at the two ends of it of one piece with the mercy seat. And the cherubim shall stretch out their wings above, covering the mercy seat with their wings, and they shall face one another; the faces of the cherubim shall be toward the mercy seat (Exodus 25:18-20, NKJV).

Again, Scripture does not explain much regarding these objects, but it is possible to draw some conclusions. Aaron's rod probably symbolized authority and leadership (see Numbers 16; 17), and the pot of manna could have symbolized God's sustaining care for Israel. The tablets of stone, of course, represented the law of God, the divine standard for judgment—while the mercy seat represented God's mercy. In this second apartment, judgment took place, so here God's justice (the law) and mercy (the mercy seat) met.

The two cherubim over the ark symbolized the heavenly host's interest in the plan of redemption. Ellen White writes:

The cherubim of the earthly sanctuary, looking reverently down upon the mercy seat, represent the interest with which the heavenly host contemplate the work of redemption. This is the mystery of mercy into which angels desire to look—that God can be just while He justifies the repenting sinner and renews His intercourse with the fallen race.[1]

The following chapters will look closely at the service in the Most Holy Place. For now, the important point is that this second apartment symbolized judgment. Here, the priest ministered during the great Day of Atonement, the earthly type of the investigative judgment. In Jewish thought, the Day of Atonement is the day of judgment, when every case is decided for life or for death. Fascinating parallels exist between the Jewish understanding of the Day of Atonement and the sections of *The Great Controversy* in which Ellen White describes the investigative judgment.[2] The similarities should not be surprising since the Jewish ritual in the Most Holy Place foreshadows the real Day of Atonement which began in heaven in 1844.

Now we return to the initial question asked in the last chapter: "Will anything—besides the cross and the character of God's people—be involved in answering questions about the character of God?" The answer is revealed, quite graphically, by the location of those two cherubim, which, according to Ellen White, "represent the interest with which the heavenly host contemplate the work of redemption."

Where are these angels found? On the altar of burnt offering, with their faces pointing down toward the sacrifice, which represents the cross? No! Instead, they have been placed all the way in the Most Holy Place, the symbol of the investigative judgment. Not at Calvary, but at the judgment seat. These cherubim represent the "ten thousand times ten thousand [that] stood before him [the Lord]" in Daniel's vision of the investigative judgment (see Daniel 7). This location makes sense when we recognize that the universe's questions about sin, the law, and the character of God were not all answered at the cross, the first phase in the plan of salvation. Not until the judgment, the final phase, will their questions be answered. "The Lord of hosts shall be exalted in judgment" (Isaiah 5:16)[3]. This is why those cherubim were placed where the judgment happens, not where the sacrifice occurs.[4]

The book of Revelation teaches this concept too. Chapter 14 gives the first angel's message, which includes the cry that "the hour of His [God's] judgment has come" (verse 7, NKJV). The time context places this judgment prior to the end of the world because the two angels that follow the first warn about future events—the fall of Babylon and the mark of the beast—that immediately precede the second coming of Jesus. Therefore, this judgment cry of the first angel must begin before Jesus returns.

In chapter 16, we have the outpouring of the seven last plagues. These, too, precede the second coming. "I heard a loud voice from the temple saying to the seven angels, 'Go and pour out the bowls of the wrath of God on the earth' " (verse 1, NKJV). The rest of the chapter deals with the plagues, beginning with "a foul and loathsome sore . . . upon the men who had the mark of the beast and those who worshiped his image" (verse 2, NKJV), and ending with "a great earthquake, such . . . as had not occurred since men were on the earth" (verse 18). When the plagues begin in chapter 16, probation must have already closed, with each case decided for life or for death. Therefore, the judgment announced in Revelation 14 must have ended by the time the plagues begin in chapter 16.

Meanwhile, as the plagues are being poured out (but only after the judgment proclaimed in chapter 14 has been finished), an angel cries out: " 'Even so, Lord God Almighty, true and righteous are Your judgments' " (Revelation 16:7, NKJV). How does the angel know that God's judgments are righteous? Because the angels have been witnesses to the judgment. "Thou art righteous, O Lord, which art, and wast, and shalt be, because thou hast judged thus" (Revelation 16:5).

Revelation 15 links the plagues with the judgment in the heavenly sanctuary. "After these things I looked in heaven and behold, the temple of the tabernacle of the testimony in heaven was opened. And out of the temple came the seven angels having the seven plagues" (verses 5, 6). These angels, who bring the plagues, come out of the temple, where the investigative judgment has been held. Apparently, the judgment in the temple has ended, and now the angels, having left the heavenly edifice, release these horrible scourges upon mankind. They have been witnesses to the judgment and have seen for themselves just how fair and just God has been; they can still praise God and His judgments as "righteous and true," even though the plagues devastate the earth.

In order to comprehend the investigative judgment, we must keep in mind the cosmic panorama. God doesn't need the investigative judgment in order to know who is saved or lost any more than He needed Abraham to slay Isaac on Mount Moriah in order to know Abraham's faith. "The Lord knoweth them that are his" (2 Timothy 2:19). The rest of the universe, however, didn't know Abraham's heart. The sinless intelligences of the unfallen worlds are not omniscient, and therefore the Lord will deal with sin in a way that will forever answer their questions. "In the judgment of the universe," writes Ellen White, "God will stand clear of blame for the existence or continuance of evil."[5] When the investigative judgment is finished, the universe will have more of their questions answered.

There is still another reason the universe is so interested in the judgment. When the redeemed begin their seven-day journey across the cosmos to the city of God to live forever in the presence of sinless beings, will King David—an adulterer and murderer—be there? What about Aaron, who made the golden calf for Israel to worship? What about the endless thousands who, even while converted, have fallen into serious sins? The universe needs reassurance that these individuals will not begin stirring up heaven with sin once again. Those who do not accept God's salvation will definitely be excluded from heaven. "He that believeth not is condemned already" (John 3:18). Yet, among those who will be saved are those who have done evil, not merely before their conversion, but afterward as well. No wonder they need Jesus to be both their substitutionary sacrifice and also their High Priest. He is also able to save to the uttermost those who come to God through Him, since He ever lives to make intercession for them" (Hebrews 7:25, NKJV). He's interceding in their behalf because even though they are God's people, even though they have their names written in the book of life, they have still sinned against Him. "If anyone sins, we have an Advocate with the Father, Jesus Christ the righteous" (1 John 2:1, NKJV). Yet some of these people will live forever in heaven in the presence of sinless beings. Could the universe be a bit nervous about such a prospect?

A few weeks after my conversion, I joked with my Adventist friends, "The first thing I'm going to do when I get to heaven is start a rebellion!" Aghast, they told me to get on my knees and repent, which I did. Through the grace of God, I have been overcoming my frivolity. But you can be sure, as I am, that when my names comes up in the judgment, the onlooking universe will want assurance that I won't, indeed, start a rebellion.

God knows our hearts and our motives. He knows those who are "safe to save." But the sinless beings of the unfallen worlds don't, which is why every case examined in the pre-advent judgment is judged before the intense scrutiny of the onlooking universe. And when it's over, the universe's questions will be so sufficiently answered that its unfallen inhabitants will shout praises to God for His fairness and justice in His dealing with human beings. "Even so, Lord God Almighty, true and righteous are Your judgments" (Revelation 16:7, NKJV). "Thou art righteous, O Lord, which art, and wast, and shalt be, because thou hast judged thus" (Revelation 16:5).

---

1. *The Great Controversy*, p. 415.
2. For a fuller study on the Jewish conception of the Day of Atonement, see *1844 Made Simple*, pages 39, 40. Also, any Jewish prayer book for the Day of Atonement reveals the Jewish understanding of what happens. Numerous parallels to the Adventist understanding of the investigative judgment can clearly be seen.
3. "The deepest interest manifested among men in the decisions of earthly tribunals but faintly represents the interest evinced in the heavenly courts when the names entered in the book of life come up in review before the Judge of all the earth" (*The Great Controversy*, pp. 483, 484).
4. It's true that cherubim were embroidered on curtains inside the Holy Place, but this is not as forceful a representation of what they mean as are the two gold ones in the second apartment.
5. *The Desire of Ages*, p. 58.

Chapter **10**

# Through a Glass Darkly

**W**e have just said, in the preceding chapter, that the investigative judgment is for the unfallen universe which has the books opened before them (see Daniel 7). What about us, the professed followers of Christ? Don't we, too, have questions? Who doesn't wrestle with painful gaps in understanding? Even living in the end time amid a blaze of light and truth not seen since Jesus Himself walked on earth in the flesh, we struggle with incidents we don't understand. We have questions we wish were answered, which might even cause us to doubt the "manifold wisdom of God."

"Now we see through a glass, darkly; but then face to

face: now I know in part; but then shall I know even as also I am known" (1 Corinthians 13:12).

Paul says that we have clouded vision now, that we don't understand things fully. Considering that the great controversy deals with infinite issues that affect the far reaches of the cosmos, it's hardly surprising that we, with sin-wracked, finite minds, see only through "a glass, darkly." One day, however, we will see "face to face." So much light and understanding will be revealed to us that eventually we, as Paul, "Shall know . . . even as . . . [we are] known." As clear as Paul's life is to the heavenly intelligences, that's how clear the issues one day will be to him—and to us.

In 1 Corinthians 4:5, Paul says that we are to judge nothing "until the Lord come, who both will bring to light the hidden things of darkness, and will make manifest the counsels of the hearts." The Lord's coming will inaugurate the millennial reign in heaven, which, according to the Bible, is when the redeemed will reign as judges:

> He laid hold of the dragon, that serpent of old, who is the Devil and Satan, and bound him for a thousand years. . . . And I saw thrones, and they sat on them, and judgment was committed to them. And I saw the souls of those who had been beheaded for their witness to Jesus and for the word of God, who had not worshiped the beast or his image, and had not received his mark on their foreheads or on their hands. And they lived and reigned with Christ for a thousand years (Revelation 20:2, 4, NKJV).

During this time, the saints (the same ones who, according to Daniel 7, receive the kingdom after the investigative judgment)[1] will be judging, not just men, but fallen angels too. "Do you not know that the saints will judge the world? And if the world will be judged by you, are you unworthy to judge the smallest matters? Do you not know that we shall judge angels?" (1 Corinthians 6:2, 3).

This judgment can occur only during the millennium, when we will have our questions answered as we study for a thousand years the issues in the great controversy—especially concerning the unredeemed, who are awaiting their final punishment. Obviously, great light must be given us, otherwise how can we be fair judges? "In union with Christ," writes Ellen White of the millennial judgment, "they [the redeemed] judge the wicked, comparing their acts with the statute book, the Bible, and deciding every case according to the deeds done in the body. Then the portion which the wicked must suffer is meted out, according to their works; and it is recorded against their names in the book of death."[2] Indeed, this judgment does for us what the investigative judgment does for the onlooking universe. It answers our questions.

Yet God is still not through. So far, the unfallen intelligences of the universe, as well as redeemed humanity, have had their questions answered. But what about the unredeemed, the fallen angels, and Satan himself?

After the millennium, the unsaved are resurrected. Together with Satan and his fallen angels (who have remained quarantined on the desolated earth during the thousand years), they stand before the Lord. He displays before them the fall of Adam and then the successive steps in the plan of redemption, especially the life of Christ and His death on the cross.[3] Then as the books of record are opened, the unsaved become conscious of every sin as they stand before their Maker and Judge without excuse.

"It is now evident to all," writes Ellen White, "that the wages of sin is not noble independence and eternal life, but slavery, ruin, and death. The wicked see what they have forfeited by their life of rebellion. . . . All see that their exclusion from heaven is just."[4] Even Satan himself, when confronted with the fruit of his rebellion, admits that God has been just and fair, and that he deserves the sentence pronounced upon him.

Satan sees that his voluntary rebellion has unfitted him for heaven. He has trained his powers to war against God; the purity, peace, and harmony of heaven would be to him supreme torture. His accusations against the mercy and justice of God are now silenced. The reproach which he has endeavored to cast upon Jehovah rests wholly upon himself. And now Satan bows down and confesses the justice of his sentence.[5]

Everyone, even Satan, confesses the righteousness of God.

Every question of truth and error in the long-standing controversy has now been made plain. . . . The working out of Satan's rule in contrast with the government of God has been presented to the

94

whole universe. Satan's own works have condemned him. God's wisdom, His justice, and His goodness stand fully vindicated. . . . With all the facts of the great controversy in view, the whole universe, both loyal and rebellious, with one accord declare: 'Just and true are Thy ways, Thou King of saints.' "[6]

We see essentially three phases of judgment: the investigative (for the benefit of the unfallen universe), the millennial (for the benefit of the redeemed), and the executive (for the benefit of the lost).

Yet the judgment most pertinent to us now is the investigative. Numerous questions remain, especially for those who face it. The following chapters continue to look at this judgment. With a proper understanding of it, we—though still seeing "through a glass, darkly"—can nevertheless confidently shout, even now, "Just and true are Thy ways, Thou King of saints!"

---

1. "The kingdom and dominion, and the greatness of the kingdom under the whole heaven, shall be given to the people of the saints of the most High" (Daniel 7:27).
2. *The Great Controversy*, p. 661.
3. See *The Great Controversy*, chapter 42.
4. Ibid., p. 668.
5. Ibid., p. 670.
6. Ibid., pp. 670, 671.

# Chapter 11

# The First Law of Heaven

Years ago in Atlanta, I chatted on the sidewalk with a man who was studying recombinant DNA.

"Looking as closely as you have at the essence of life itself," I asked, "don't you see evidence for the existence of God?"

"Wherever you look," he answered, "whether outward into the universe or inward into the minutest detail of a cell, you see one common thing—order."

Instantly, a quote from Ellen White bobbed into my mind: "Order is heaven's first law."[1]

Order! God, indeed, does everything in order. The Creation account: day one, day two, day three—this made, then this, and then this. Everything in order. Jesus, after

He fed the 5,000, told His awed disciples to "gather up the fragments that remain, so that nothing is lost" (John 6:12, NKJV). After the resurrection, the disciples rushed to the gravesite, finding it empty, though by the tomb were Christ's graveclothes, "not thrown heedlessly aside, but carefully folded, each in a place by itself."[2] Why? Because, as Ellen White explains, "in His sight who guides alike the star and the atom, there is nothing unimportant. Order and perfection are seen in all His work."[3]

All that God does is marked by order. In the books of Exodus and Leviticus, when the Lord instructed the Israelites about the construction and function of the earthly tabernacle, everything was in strict order. From construction of furniture to the sacrifices, God mandated that everything be done in a specific, orderly fashion. In the construction of the lampstand, for instance, the Lord told Moses:

> "You shall . . . make a lampstand of pure gold; the lampstand shall be of hammered work. Its shaft, its branches, it bowls, its ornamental knobs, and flowers shall be of one piece. And six branches shall come out of its sides: three branches of the lampstand out of one side, and three branches of the lampstand out of the other side. Three bowls shall be made like almond blossoms on one branch, with an ornamental knob and a flower, and three bowls made like almond blossoms on the other branch, with an ornamental knob and a flower—and so for the six branches that come out of the lampstand. On the lampstand itself four bowls shall be made like almond blossoms, each with its ornamental knob and flower. And there shall be a knob

under the first two branches of the same" (Exodus 25:31-35, NKJV).

All through the instructions for the construction of the sanctuary, the Lord told them, "See . . . that you make them according to the pattern which was shown you on the mountain" (Exodus 25:40, NKJV). Why? Because God is a God of order.

How does this specific aspect of God's character relate to the investigative judgment?

Past chapters have shown that the entire intelligent universe is intensely interested in the problems of sin and rebellion. Though restricted to the earth now, sin is a universal issue, and God intends to eradicate it in a manner that will satisfy all the universe, including mankind, redeemed and unredeemed.

Previous chapters have shown also that God has different steps in resolving the great controversy and that the earthly sanctuary symbolized these steps, beginning with Jesus on the cross (the altar of burnt offerings), and ending with the judgment (the Most Holy Place). Though the cross answered many questions for the universe, God still intends to use other factors, such as the character of His people and the investigative judgment, to help resolve all the issues.

Now, the point is this: Christ's death on the cross and His high priestly ministry in heaven (both in the Holy and Most Holy Places) are part of God's *orderly* way of disposing of sin and evil from the universe. Christ's death and ministry are part of God's *orderly* way of casting our sins into the "depths of the sea" without casting us in as well. Christ's death and heavenly ministry are part of God's *orderly* way of dealing with, and finally resolving, the problem of sin, as well as answering all the questions about His character that these problems have raised.

How?

Talking about Jesus, Hebrews 9:28 says, "Unto them that look for him shall he appear the second time without sin unto salvation." What does it mean, "without sin"? This text implies that Jesus had sin, but when He returns He won't still have it. Did Jesus ever sin?

Of course not!

"We have not an high priest which cannot be touched with the feeling of our infirmities; but was in all points tempted like as we are, yet without sin" (Hebrews 4:15).

"Who did no sin, neither was guile found in his mouth" (1 Peter 2:22).

"Forasmuch as ye know that ye were not redeemed with corruptible things, as silver and gold, from your vain conversation received by tradition from your fathers; but with the precious blood of Christ, as of a lamb without blemish and without spot" (1 Peter 1:18, 19).

In this last verse, Peter alludes to the sacrificial animals in the earthly sanctuary services. They symbolized Jesus, which is why the lamb had to be "without spot or blemish." Jesus needed to be perfect—without fault or sin—in order to meet the demands of the law.

Jesus never sinned. But did He ever *have* sin?

"Christ was once offered to bear the sins of many; and unto them that look for him shall he appear the second time without sin unto salvation" (Hebrews 9:28).

"Who his own self bare our sins in his own body on the tree" (1 Peter 2:24).

"The Lord has laid on him the iniquity of us all" (Isaiah 53:6).

On that cross, not only did Jesus bear sin, He became sin! "He hath made him to be sin for us, who knew no sin; that we might be made the righteousness of God in him" (2 Corinthians 5:21).

Jesus, with no sin of His own, took our sins, bore them in His body, and even became sin for us. The sins of the world fell on Him to the point that they crushed out His life. Calvary is phase one of God's plan to eradicate sin from the universe without having to eradicate sinners as well.

What happens next?

"As anciently the sins of the people were by faith placed upon the sin offering and through its blood transferred, in figure, to the earthly sanctuary," writes Ellen White, "so in the new covenant the sins of the repentant are by faith placed upon Christ and transferred, in fact, to the heavenly sanctuary."[4]

If we look at the earthly system as a parable of the real plan of salvation involving the heavenly sanctuary, then sin has to be transferred into the heavenly sanctuary. That is why the Bible (see Hebrews 9:23) and the Spirit of Prophecy speak of the sanctuary needing to be cleansed.[5] This transfer of sin becomes clearer when we understand Christ's high priestly ministry in the heavenly sanctuary.

"Who is he that condemneth? It is Christ that died, yea rather, that is risen again, who is even at the right hand of God, who also maketh intercession for us" (Romans 8:34).

"He is able also to save them to the uttermost that come unto God by him, seeing he ever liveth to make intercession for them" (Hebrews 7:25).

"Christ came as High Priest of the good things to come, with the greater and more perfect tabernacle not made with hands, that is, not of this creation" (Hebrews 9:11, NKJV).

Jesus, who was our Lamb on the earth, dying for the sins of the world, is now our High Priest, making "intercession for us" in the "true tabernacle," the one in heaven.

"If he were on earth, he would not be a priest at all, since there are priests who offer gifts according to the law. They serve a copy and shadow of the heavenly sanctuary (Hebrews 8:4, 5, RSV).

The Bible is explicit: a literal, physical sanctuary exists in heaven. Attempts have been made to undermine the investigative judgment doctrine by denying the reality of the heavenly sanctuary and emphasizing Christ's *work* in heaven at the expense of the location of that work. Of course, what He is doing is more important than where. But no need exists to downplay, or deny, the literalness of the structure in heaven in order to emphasize Christ's ministry. On the contrary, only by understanding that the sanctuary is literal can one truly grasp Christ's ministry in it.[6]

Hebrews say unequivocally that the earthly system was merely a "shadow" or a "copy" of the heavenly. Which is more *real,* an object or the ethereal shadow it casts? Of course, the object itself. The Bible calls the literal earthly sanctuary—with gold, wood, animal skins, fire, water, and blood—just a "shadow," an "image" of the heavenly. Surely the heavenly reality must be as literal at least as the earthly shadow.

"Christ is not entered into the holy places made with hands [the earthly sanctuary], which are the figures of the true; but into heaven itself, now to appear in the presence of God for us" (Hebrews 9:24).

Jesus is ministering in a literal sanctuary in heaven, standing at the right hand of God as High Priest, and making intercession for His people. But what does "making intercession" entail? He's mediating for us, but what is mediation? He's a priest, but what does a priest do?

Though the Bible doesn't give precise detail about Christ's work in heaven, it does say that the ministry of the earthly priesthood in the sanctuary was a "figure," or a "shadow," of what happens in heaven. Therefore, a look at the earthly, which is detailed, helps reveal the heavenly.

The earthly sanctuary parallels the heavenly in a number of ways:

| Earthly | Heavenly |
| --- | --- |
| 1. Lamb (animal) | Lamb (Jesus) |
| 2. Priest (Levites) | Priest (Jesus) |
| 3. Blood (animal blood) | Blood (Jesus' blood) |
| 4. Sin | Sin |
| 5. Sinners | Sinners |
| 6. Sanctuary (made with hands) | Sanctuary (made by God) |

The difference is that instead of earthly priests, the heavenly sanctuary has Jesus as priest; instead of animals, Jesus' sacrifice precedes the priestly ministration; instead of animal blood, the blood in the heavenly sanctuary is Christ's blood; and instead of an earthly sanctuary made with hands, it's now a heavenly sanctuary, "the true tabernacle, which God pitched, and not man."

103

Obviously, the heavenly sacrifice and ministration are better than the earthly, and a good part of the book of Hebrews is devoted to teaching that specific point.[7]

The next chapter looks at what happens in the earthly service and what it can teach us about the heavenly.

---

1. *Testimonies for the Church,* vol. 6, p. 201.

2. *The Desire of Ages,* p. 789.

3. Ibid.

4. *The Great Controversy,* p. 42.

5. The details of this aspect of the plan of salvation are not entirely clear. If we press the type, making a one-to-one correlation, then when He ascended into heaven, Jesus must have taken sin with Him, thus defiling the sanctuary with His blood. Nothing in Scripture, however, or in Ellen White's writings, specifically says that. Hebrews deals with Christ's blood only in the context of cleansing (see 9:23), though in the earthly system, it seems that clean blood cleansed and that defiled blood defiled. Therefore, as Christ was our sin bearer on the cross, His blood would have been defiled, defiling the sanctuary. Another explanation is that the sin, or at least its record, enters the sanctuary when we commit the act and is marked in the books. Though more study needs to be done, the crucial point is that "sin" is transferred into the heavenly sanctuary. Also, we must remember that the earthly sanctuary service was meant to give only the broad picture of the plan of salvation, not minor details.

6. "This issue is significant for the Seventh-day Adventist church," writes William Johnsson, "when we recall the place that a *realistic* heavenly sanctuary and ministry have in our heritage. Our pioneers and Ellen White long ago looked to the book of Hebrews as strong support for an actual heavenly sanctuary and an actual heavenly work by Jesus Christ, our actual High Priest. To dissolve these realities into metaphorical speech must surely transform Seventh-day Adventist doctrine." Frank Holbrook, ed., *Issues in the Book of Hebrews* (Silver Spring, Md.: Biblical Research Institute, 1989), pp. 37, 38.

7. All the way through the book of Hebrews, the theme of the superiority of the heavenly ministry over the earthly is apparent. There is a better revelation (1:1-4); a better name (1:5–2:18); a better leader (3:1–4:16); a better priest (5:1–6:20); a better priesthood (7:1-27); a better sanctuary (8:1-6); a better covenant (8:7-13); a better sacrifice (9:1–10:18). See Frank Holbrook, ed., *Issues in the Book of Hebrews,* pp. 13-35.

# Chapter 12

# The First Law of Heaven (Cont.)

The earthly sanctuary dealt with penitent sinners only, those acknowledging their sin and seeking forgiveness. Those who came to the sanctuary unprepared were "cut off from among the people." If, however, a person committed a sin, was sorry, and sought forgiveness, a special ritual took place. (The exact ritual depended upon who sinned and what sin he committed.) "The only sin transferred to the sanctuary was the sin of one who humbled himself before the Lord, asked forgiveness, and brought a sacrifice."[1]

What basic ritual dealt with sin?

The Lord spoke to Moses, saying, "Speak to the children of Israel, saying . . . 'If a person sins unintentionally against any of the commandments of the Lord in anything which ought not to be done, and does any of them, if the anointed priest sins, bringing guilt on the people, then let him offer to the Lord for his sin which he has sinned a young bull without blemish as a sin offering. He shall bring the bull to the door of the tabernacle of meeting before the Lord, lay his hand on the bull's head, and kill the bull before the Lord. Then the anointed priest shall take some of the bull's blood and bring it to the tabernacle of meeting' " (Leviticus 4:1-5, NKJV).

The significance of laying hands upon the animal is clearly explained only once in the context of the sanctuary service, in this case dealing with the Day of Atonement scapegoat:

Aaron shall lay both his hands upon the head of the live goat, and confess over him all the iniquities of the children of Israel, and all their transgressions in all their sins, putting them upon the head of the goat, and shall send him away by the hand of a fit man into the wilderness: and the goat shall bear upon him all their iniquities (Leviticus 16:21, 22).

The symbolism is clear: laying hands upon the animal symbolically transferred sin, putting them upon the goat. In contexts other than the sanctuary, laying hands on someone represents transference of other nontangible things. When Joshua, son of Nun, became the leader in Israel, the Lord said to Moses, " 'Take

Joshua the son of Nun . . . a man in whom is the Spirit, and lay your hand on him; set him before Eleazer the priest and before all the congregation, and inaugurate him in their sight. And you shall give some of your authority to him, that all the congregation of the children of Israel may be obedient' " (Numbers 27:18-20, NKJV).

When the Levites were consecrated to the priesthood to become spiritual leaders and ministers in the sanctuary, authority and responsibility were transferred to them.[2] "So you shall bring the Levites before the Lord, and the children of Israel shall lay their hands on the Levites" (Numbers 8:10, NKJV).

In the context of the sacrificial system, however, laying hands on the sacrificial animal symbolized the transfer of sin from the guilty sinner to the innocent animal, in the same way that our sins were transferred to Jesus at Calvary. Imagine placing your hands on the bloodied head of Jesus on the cross and confessing your sin over Him! That idea, essentially, is what the sacrificial service symbolized. "The Lord has laid on Him the iniquity of us all" (Isaiah 53:6, NKJV). Jesus took in reality what the animal received only in symbol.

After the animal was killed, its blood was brought into the precincts of the earthly sanctuary. Who brought it there? The sinner? No, he wasn't allowed to enter the sanctuary. The animal? No, it was dead. The officiating priest alone could intercede in behalf of the sinner by bringing the blood into the sanctuary.

In another sanctuary ritual, Moses says to two priests, Eleazar and Ithamar, sons of Aaron, "Wherefore ye have not eaten the sin offering in the holy place . . . [for] God hath given it you to bear the iniquity of the congregation, to make atonement for before the Lord? Behold, the blood of it was not brought in within the holy place" (Leviticus 10:17, 18).

A repentant sinner brought his sacrifice to the sanctuary. He placed his hands upon the animal's head and confessed his sin. The sin was then "transferred" to the innocent animal, which was killed instead of the sinner. The priest then took the blood and sprinkled it on the altar of burnt offering or in the sanctuary itself, or the priest himself ate the meat of the offering. Thus he made "atonement" for the sinner. In symbol, the sin was transferred to the sanctuary by the priest.

In the above passages, the priests were to "bear the iniquity" (*nasa 'awon*) of the congregation. The word *nasa* comes from a common Hebrew root used hundreds of times meaning literally "to bear," "to carry," "to lift." *Nasa,* however, has been translated another way. After Israel had sinned by making and worshiping the golden calf, Moses pleaded in behalf of his wayward people before the Lord. Now, if You will forgive their sin—but if not, I pray, blot me out of Your book which You have written" (Exodus 32:32, NKJV). The word translated "forgive" is taken from *nasa.* What Moses says to the Lord, then, is literally: "Now, if You will *bear* their sin—but if not, I pray, blot me out of the book which You have written." When Moses returned to Mount Sinai after the golden calf apostasy, the Lord passed before him and proclaimed: "The Lord, the Lord God, merciful and gracious, longsuffering, and abundant in goodness and truth, keeping mercy for thousands, forgiving [from *nasa*] iniquity and transgression and sin" (Exodus 34:6).

In more than a dozen verses in Scripture, *nasa* is translated as "forgive" or "pardon." These verses convey the idea that the sinner receives forgiveness when someone else—such as a priest (see Leviticus 10:17, 18) or even God (see Exodus 32:32; 34:6) or a High Priest who is God (see Hebrews 8:1)—bears his sin instead of the sinner bearing it himself.[3]

This substitution is how we receive forgiveness. God cannot simply ignore sin. The penalty must be paid, if not by the sinner, then by a substitute. If there is no substitute, then as Leviticus 5:1 says, the sinner is to bear his iniquity himself.

The concept of substitution forms the basis of atonement in Jewish thought. "In every sacrifice," says *The Jewish Encyclopedia,* "there is the idea of substitution; the victim takes the place of the human sinner. The laying of hands upon the victim's head is an ordinary rite by which the substitution and transfer of sins are effected."[4]

In the sanctuary service, a sinner came to the entrance of the courtyard with his spotless sacrifice. Placing a hand upon the head of the animal, he confessed his sin, "transferring" it to the substitute, which then died instead of the sinner. Its blood, which now "contained" the sin, was picked up by the priest, who for the moment bore the iniquity of the sinner, until he brought it into the sanctuary, where it was deposited.

The Jews regarded sin as a tangible thing that went from the sinner to the animal to the priest to the sanctuary. Think of sin as a deadly virus, the blood as a vial, the priest as a special transport, and the sanctuary as a storehouse where biological weapons are temporarily deposited. The virus of sin is transferred (in the blood) by a special carrier (the priest), who brings it to the storehouse (the sanctuary), where it is kept until finally eradicated.

Meanwhile, once sin was transferred to the animal, who suffered instead of the sinner, the guilty one walked away free, pardoned, no longer bearing the guilt of the sin he had committed. The transfer of sin, as a means of allowing sinners to be forgiven the penalty of their transgression, continued daily in ancient Israel.

This earthly system, however, merely foreshadowed the true tabernacle, where Jesus Himself is now ministering as our High Priest in heaven. Right now, anyone who has confessed his sin to Jesus, in a sense laying his hands upon Christ's bloodied head and claiming the holiness that He offers to impute to us by the virtue of His perfect life, has his sin taken from him. As did the sinner in ancient Israel, he walks away forgiven, pardoned, justified. He is no longer under the condemnation of the law because Jesus paid the penalty for that broken law. "Christ has redeemed us from the curse of the law, having become a curse for us" (Galatians 3:13, NKJV). He no longer faces the guilt of his sin because Jesus took it upon Himself instead. The Lord has laid on Him the iniquity of us all" (Isaiah 53:6, NKJV). And he no longer faces the penalty of his transgression because Jesus faced it for him by becoming the sin-bearer Himself, both as sacrifice and as priest. "Being justified freely by His grace through the redemption that is in Christ Jesus, whom God set forth to be a propitiation by His blood" (Romans 3:24, 25, NKJV).

In the ritual, what ultimately happened to the sin after the priest carried it into the earthly sanctuary? The answer is found in what happened on the Day of Atonement when the sanctuary itself was cleansed.

---

1. Frank Holbrook, ed., *Seventy Weeks, Leviticus, Nature of Prophecy* (Washington, D.C.: Biblical Research Institute, 1986), p. 196.

2. For a deeper study on this whole concept of laying on of hands, see *Seventy Weeks, Leviticus, Nature of Prophecy,* pp. 180-183.

3. For a fuller study of the phrase *nasa 'awon,* see Clifford Goldstein, "Who Shall Atone for Us?" *Shabbat Shalom* (October-December 1989), pp. 8-11.

4. *The Jewish Encyclopedia* (New York: Funk and Wagnells, 1902), vol. 2, p. 276.

# Chapter 13

# The Cleansing of the Sanctuary

T alking about the sanctuary, Leviticus 16:19 says that the priest shall "cleanse it, and sanctify it from the uncleanness of the children of Israel" (NKJV).

How could the sanctuary be defiled by the children of Israel, when the people weren't even allowed to enter? Though they could never go into the sanctuary, their sins were "carried" there in the blood by the priests. The priest deposited the sin, symbolized by the "defiled" blood, in the sanctuary itself. Once a year, however, the accumulation of sin was transferred again, this time removed from the sanctuary. In this service, the sanctuary was "cleansed." Sin was removed from the camp entirely, a shadow of how God intends to remove sin from the universe.

113

In the same way he [Moses] sprinkled both the tabernacle and all the vessels of the ministry with the blood. And according to the Law, one may almost say, all things are cleansed with blood, and without shedding of blood there is no forgiveness. Therefore it was necessary for the copies of the things in the heavens [the earthly sanctuary] to be cleansed with these, but the heavenly things themselves with better sacrifices than these. For Christ did not enter a holy place made with hands, a mere copy of the true one, but into heaven itself, now to appear in the presence of God for us (Hebrews 9:21-24, NASB).

The context of Daniel 8:14 ("Unto two thousand and three hundred days; then shall the sanctuary be cleansed") reveals that it can refer only to the heavenly sanctuary and the cleansing process that it goes through at the appointed time.[1]

Why would the sanctuary in heaven need cleansing? Because of our sins which were brought there. Under the new covenant, inaugurated at the death of Jesus, sin goes from the sinner to Jesus, first as sacrifice (lamb), then as High Priest, and finally into the heavenly sanctuary, which needs to be cleansed as a result.[2]

Eventually, however, Jesus will no longer be our High Priest ministering in the sanctuary. For this reason, when He comes the second time, it will be "without sin" (Hebrews 9:28). He no longer bears sin as the High Priest once the sanctuary is cleansed and sin is transferred to Satan (see below). In the same manner, the high priest in the Old Testament service no longer bore sin once the earthly sanctuary was cleansed and sin had been transferred to the scapegoat.

Various places in Leviticus talk about a sinner bringing an animal to be sacrificed in order that "the priest shall make an atonement for him." This phrase is repeated throughout the book of Leviticus.[3] These people needed atonement because they had sinned. Thanks to the sacrificial system, a way had been made to separate them from their sin and thus provide forgiveness. We can understand how sinners need an atonement to be made for them.

But what does Leviticus 16:15, 16 mean? "He shall kill the goat of the sin offering, which is for the people, bring its blood inside the veil, do with that blood as he did with the blood of the bull, and sprinkle it on the mercy seat and before the mercy seat. *So he shall make atonement for the Holy Place*" (emphasis supplied, NKJV).

An atonement for the Holy Place? People sin. People break the law. People need atonement. But a building? Why would a building, an inanimate structure, need atonement?

"He shall make an atonement for the holy place, because of the uncleanness of the children of Israel, and because of their transgressions in all their sins" (Leviticus 16:16).

Why does the sanctuary need atonement? Because of *all* the transgressions of the children of Israel, which day after day were brought into the sanctuary by the priests. Sin was removed from the sinner and deposited in the sanctuary (remember the virus imagery). Just as sin defiled the sinner, it ultimately defiled the sanctuary when deposited there via the blood. "The fact that during the Day of Atonement the sanctuary was cleansed from all the sins of the people of Israel," writes scholar Angel M. Rodriguez, "suggests that the sin of the people was transferred, in the person of the priest, to the sanctuary."[4]

On one day each year, the Day of Atonement, the sanctuary itself was atoned for. Just as atonement for a sinner involved the removal of sin from the person himself, atonement for the sanctuary involved the removal of sin from the building itself.

The sanctuary process had two main phases: the first apartment ministry, a daily, ongoing process that brought sin into the sanctuary, and the second apartment ministry, the Day of Atonement, that brought the sin out. On the Day of Atonement, which is the Day of Judgment in Jewish thought (also known as the "Day of Purifications"), animals were killed and their blood brought into the sanctuary as in the daily ritual. But crucial differences existed between the Day of Atonement rituals and the daily sacrifices. First, on the Day of Atonement, blood was brought into the *second* apartment, the Most Holy Place, and sprinkled before the mercy seat behind the second veil. At no other time was blood brought there.

A second difference, noted by Adventist as well as non-Adventist scholars, is that no mention is made of hands being laid upon the goat that was offered on the Day of Atonement. No mention is made of sin being confessed upon it.

He shall kill the goat of the sin offering, which is

for the people, bring its blood inside the veil [the veil before the second apartment], do with that blood as he did with the blood of the bull, and sprinkle it on the mercy seat and before the mercy seat. So he shall make atonement for the Holy Place, because of the uncleanness of the children of Israel, and because of their transgressions, for all their sins (Leviticus 16:15, 16, NKJV).

In other words, the blood brought into the Most Holy Place to make atonement for the sanctuary did not have sin in it as did the blood in the daily service. It was, in a sense, "clean blood." It has been suggested that this "clean blood" picked up all the sins accumulated in the sanctuary during the year. Using the virus analogy, a clean, empty vial (the clean blood) was brought into the storehouse (the sanctuary), where it picked up the virus (the sin) and took it out, thus "cleansing" the sanctuary. "The daily rituals transferred sin and impurity to the sanctuary," writes scholar Alberto Treiyer, and "the yearly ritual (Day of Atonement) removed this deposit away from the sanctuary."[5]

In the Day of Atonement ritual, after atonement has been made for the sanctuary with the "clean" blood of the goat (remember, atonement involves the transfer of sin), a second goat is introduced into the service. The High Priest "shall lay both his hands"—bloodied from sprinkling the blood—"upon the head of the live goat, and confess over him all the iniquities of the children of Israel, and all their transgressions in all their sins, putting them upon the head of the goat, and shall send him away by the hand of a fit man and into the wilderness: the goat shall bear upon him all their iniquities unto a land not inhabited" (Leviticus 16:21, 22).

The sequence is clear: sin went from the sinner to the animal through the confession of sin and the laying on of hands. The animal was then killed, and the priest, via the defiled blood, deposited the sin in the sanctuary. On the Day of Atonement, the priest then brought in clean blood, which picked up all the sin (it then became sin-laden blood), and then all that sin was placed on the head of the scapegoat, which was sent into the wilderness. Thus sin, which began with the sinner, was finally brought outside the camp, and the result was that the sanctuary, the camp, and the people were cleansed.

Much elaboration (and speculation) can go into the details of the rituals. What we need to look at here is the transfer of sin. In the sanctuary service, sin didn't just vanish. It wasn't just forgiven and then forgotten. Instead, the Lord developed an elaborate ritual to symbolize the process by which sin is removed in reality.

As anciently the sins of the people were by faith placed upon the sin offering and through its blood transferred, in figure, to the earthly sanctuary, so in the new covenant the sins of the repentant are by faith placed upon Christ and transferred, in fact, to the heavenly sanctuary. And as the typical cleansing of the earthly was accomplished by the removal of the sins by which it had been polluted, so the actual cleansing of the heavenly is to be accomplished by the removal, or blotting out, of the sins which are there recorded.[6]

The cleansing of sin from the earthly temple was an illustration of the cleansing of sin in the heavenly sanctuary: "Unto two thousand and three hundred days; then shall the sanctuary be cleansed" (Daniel 8:14). "It was therefore necessary that the patterns of things in the heavens [the heavenly sanctuary] should be purified" (Hebrews 9:23). In the earthly sanctuary, this cleansing was symbolized by the removal of sin; in the heavenly, the record of the sins will be blotted out. "Repent ye therefore, and be converted, that your sins may be blotted out" (Act 3:19). The result, either in symbol (earthly) or in reality (the heavenly), is the same—the sanctuary is cleansed.

What ultimately happens to sin after the record of it is blotted out and it leaves the sanctuary? Sin is placed on the scapegoat, who, in Jewish thought, represents the chief of the rebellious angels. Writes Ellen White:

> It was seen, also, that while the sin offering pointed to Christ as a sacrifice, and the high priest represented Christ as a mediator, the scapegoat typified Satan, the author of sin, upon whom the sins of the truly penitent will finally be placed. When the high priest, by virtue of the blood of the sin offering, removed the sins from the sanctuary, he placed them upon the scapegoat. When Christ, by virtue of His own blood, removes the sins of His people from the heavenly sanctuary at the close of His ministration, He will place them upon Satan, who, in the execution of the judgment, must bear the final penalty. The scapegoat was sent away into a land not inhabited, never to come again into the congrega-

tion of Israel. So will Satan be forever banished from the presence of God and His people, and he will be blotted from existence in the final destruction of sin and sinners.[7]

In the earthly system, sin went from the sinner to the animal to the priest to the sanctuary to the priest again, and finally to the scapegoat, sent into the wilderness by the hand of "a fit man." (Though the Bible doesn't say, the man probably had to be in good physical condition in order to lead the scapegoat so far away from the camp that it could never find its way back, an example of how far and permanently the Lord wants to remove sin from His people.) In the real sanctuary service, which the earthly system symbolized, sin goes from the sinner to Jesus as Lamb to Jesus as Priest to the heavenly sanctuary and finally to Satan, who is banished from the presence of God's people, only to be eradicated at last along with sin and sinners in the final judgment.

The Lord could have destroyed Satan the moment he rebelled. Instead, in harmony with His character of love, justice, and mercy, the Lord has chosen, at infinite cost to Himself, to dispose of sin in this step-by-step manner before the onlooking universe. In the earthly sanctuary, angels were embroidered on the wall of the first apartment; two gold cherubim sat in the Most Holy Place, the climax of the atoning process—all symbolic of the universe's interest in the plan of salvation. By an orderly, open process involving His death, and then His high-priestly ministry in a literal, physical sanctuary, the Lord will forever answer all questions regarding the great controversy and the origin of evil. The sanctuary in heaven is literal, not because God needs it, but because the heavenly intelligences need it to see how God deals with sin. By using a visible, physical structure, God allows the onlooking universe to clearly see each step in resolving the conflict.

"In the ritual type," writes Angel Rodriguez, "the penitent's confessed sin and accountability were transferred to the sanctuary through the sacrificial victim and priest. It may be said that for the time being the sanctuary assumed his guilt, and he was forgiven. On the Day of Atonement the sanctuary was cleansed, and thus God (in the sanctuary) was cleared."[8]

Important questions regarding this whole heavenly ritual remain to be answered. How does this heavenly Day of Atonement affect our lives? What does it mean for us today? The next chapter tackles these issues because what happens in the heavenly sanctuary is extremely relevant to those here on earth whose sins are recorded up there.

---

1. The time frame of that cleansing is after the activity of the horn power of the preceding verses, Daniel 8:9-12. Paralleling the description of the little horn in Daniel 8 with the activity of the little horn power in Daniel 7:8, 20, 21, 24, 25, whose persecution of the saints ended (at least temporarily) after "a time and times and half a time" (verse 25, NKJV), the time frame of the cleansing of the sanctuary extends far into the Christian dispensation, long after the earthly sanctuary has been destroyed. See Clifford Goldstein, *1844 Made Simple,* (Boise, Idaho: Pacific Press, 1988).

2. If sin is an immoral act, a deed, how can it physically be transferred somewhere, especially to the sanctuary in heaven? Yet Ellen White seems to say that sin "in fact" is transferred there (*The Great Controversy,* p. 421). Perhaps it is just the record alone, and this defiles the sanctuary? Whatever the metaphys-

# FALSE BALANCES

ics of what is happening, the important point is what it teaches about the plan of salvation.

3. See Leviticus 5:6, 10, 13, 18; 6:7; 8:34; 9:7; 14:20; 15:15; 15:30.
4. Frank Holbrook, ed., *Seventy Weeks, Leviticus, Nature of Prophecy* (Washington, D.C.: Biblical Research Institute, 1986), p. 188.
5. Ibid., p. 217.
6. *The Great Controversy*, pp. 421, 422.
7. Ibid., p. 422.
8. Frank Holbrook, ed., *Seventy Weeks, Leviticus, Nature of Prophecy*, p. 170.

Chapter **14**

# The Full and Final Display

Οn Yom Kippur, the Day of Atonement, all the sin that had daily been brought into the sanctuary by the priests through the sacrificial blood was removed and placed on the head of the scapegoat. As a result, the sanctuary was cleansed. On that day, however, not just the sanctuary was cleansed. So were the people.

This shall be a statute forever for you: In the seventh month, on the tenth day of the month, you shall afflict your souls, and do no work at all, whether a native of your own country or a stranger who sojourns among you. For on that day the priest shall make atonement for you, to cleanse you, that you may be clean from all your sins before the Lord (Leviticus 16:29, 30 NKJV).

The sanctuary structure itself was cleansed "from all the iniquities of the children of Israel," while the people themselves were to be "clean from all your sins before the Lord." Thus, this once-a-year ritual produced a clean sanctuary *and* a clean people.

"He shall make an atonement for the holy sanctuary, and he shall make an atonement for the tabernacle of the congregation, and for the altar, and he shall make an atonement for the priests, and for all the people of the congregation" (Leviticus 16:33).

Atonement came only after sin was taken away, either from an individual sinner or from the sanctuary. On Yom Kippur, atonement was made for the congregation, the priests, and the sanctuary structure itself. Sin was removed from everything.

The earthly system foreshadows the heavenly. The Levitical sacrifices, priesthood, and sanctuary were object lessons of Jesus' high-priestly ministry in the heavenly Holy of Holies. What does the special cleansing on the Day of Atonement mean for modern Israel? What does it mean for those whose sins by virtue of Christ's blood are in the heavenly sanctuary, who are now living in the great antitypical Day of Atonement when the "true tabernacle" will be cleansed?

"In the typical service," writes Ellen White, "when the high priest entered the most holy place, all Israel were required to gather about the sanctuary and in the most solemn manner humble their souls before God, that they might receive the pardon of their sins and not be cut off from the congregation. How much more essential in this antitypical Day of Atonement that we understand the work of our High Priest and know what duties are required of us."[1]

"While the investigative judgment is going forward in heaven, while the sins of penitent believers are being removed from the sanctuary, there is to be a special work of purification, of putting away of sin, among God's people upon earth."[2]

If ancient Israel, during the earthly Day of Atonement, was to be cleansed of sin, then modern Israel, in the real Day of Atonement, must be cleansed from sin as well. Hence, this "special work of purification, of putting away of sin," is an important part of what God wants to do in His people now.

Previous chapters have shown that God is dealing with the problem of sin in a manner that will answer all the questions of the onlooking universe because the issues still need to be clarified. Besides the sanctuary, the Lord is using two other factors to help clarify these questions: the character development of His people and the investigative judgment. Both these elements climax in the Day of Atonement! God will have a clean people on earth who, because they have allowed God to cleanse them from their sin, bring honor and glory to Him. Simultaneously, God is also glorified in heaven when the sanctuary is cleansed of sin during the judgment. *The Day of Atonement is the only time when both these elements happen at once in a grand and glorious climax before the onlooking universe!*

The earthly Day of Atonement was an example in

miniature of what God is going to have en masse: a clean people who glorify Him before the onlooking universe. If one person can glorify God by his character development, how much more a whole fruitful generation? What God did for His people in ancient Israel on a small scale symbolized what He wants to do for His modern people on a grand scale in the full and final display of His love. This demonstration of God's love forms the apex of the plan of salvation. Then the issues will be resolved sufficiently in the minds of the unfallen universe that God can justly pour out devastating plagues upon the rebel planet while only a short time later resurrecting and translating individuals into the presence of sinless beings.

The foundation of the entire plan of salvation was laid at the cross; the culmination of that plan is found in the cleansing of the sanctuary in heaven and the people of God on earth. What Jesus began on the cross prepared the way for what He intends to finish in the judgment. The judgment and the glorification of the redeemed could not happen without the cross. But without the judgment and the resurrection of the redeemed, what purpose would there be for the cross? The judgment leads to the glorification of the saints, which is the purpose of Christ's atonement. Only because of what Jesus did at Calvary can the saints stand in the judgment and be cleansed of all their sins. Jesus Christ is "the faithful witness, the firstborn from the dead, and the ruler over the kings of the earth. . . . Who loved us and washed us from our sins in His own blood" (Revelation 1:5, NKJV).

The three angels of Revelation 14 link judgment with a clean people. The first angel's message reads:

I saw another angel fly in the midst of heaven, having the everlasting gospel to preach unto . . . every nation, and kindred, and tongue, and people, saying with a loud voice, Fear God, and give glory to him; for the hour of his judgment is come; and worship him that made heaven, and earth, and the sea, and the fountains of waters (verse 6).

This final warning to the world, as given in Revelation 14, begins with the everlasting gospel of Christ. Thus, the cross and all that Jesus did for humanity there is depicted as the foundation of the three angels' messages. The judgment, the warning, the call to worship God, everything that follows as part of the everlasting gospel rests on the shed blood of the Son of God.

In Him we have redemption through His blood, the forgiveness of sins, according to the riches of His grace which He made to abound toward us in all wisdom and prudence . . . that in the dispensation of the fullness of the times He might gather together in one all things in Christ, both which are in heaven and which are on earth—in Him (Ephesians 1:7-10).

As shown in a previous chapter, this everlasting gospel includes the cry that "the hour of his judgment is come." The judgment is part of the gospel. While the cross and what Jesus did for us there begin the "everlasting gospel," the judgment and what Jesus does for us there finish it. A *balanced* study of the sanctuary service reveals how the cross (the altar of burnt offering) and the judgment (the Day of Atonement in the Most Holy Place) are merely different phases of the same atoning process. *The first angel is merely describing the actual manifestation of what the earthly sanctuary service had been pointing to for fifteen hundred years.*

Combined, too, with the judgment message of this first angel is the call to "fear God and give glory to Him." We give glory to God by allowing Him to sanctify us. Overcoming sin, bearing fruit, being obedient, and most important, reflecting the character of Jesus—all give honor and glory to God. This concept is an essential element of the three angels' messages; without it one cannot understand present truth.

The appeal to give glory to God is essentially a call to obedience and sanctification, and it is coupled in these verses with an emphasis on God as Creator. "Worship Him who made heaven and earth, the sea and springs of water" (NKJV). This connection is not coincidental, for God's creative power, working to renew us, gives us the characters that glorify Him.

Be renewed in the spirit of your mind, and . . . put on the new man which was created according to God, in righteousness and true holiness" (Ephesians 4:23, 24, NKJV).

"In Christ Jesus neither circumcision nor uncircumcision avails anything, but a new creation" (Galatians 6:15, NKJV).

"If anyone is in Christ, he is a new creation; old things have passed away; behold, all things have become new" (2 Corinthians 5:17, NKJV).

Only through God's creative power working on our hearts can we become new creations renewed in His image. Psalm 51:10 is usually translated, "Create in me a clean heart, O God." A more literal translation is, "A clean heart create *for* me, O God." The sanctification process is a work that God does *for* us. He first created us, but because of the damage of sin, He now is in the process of re-creating us.

Also, in Psalm 51, David asks God to wash him from his iniquity, to make him pure from his sin, and even to "blot out" his transgressions (blotting out of sin occurs in the investigative judgment) so that "thou [God] mightest be justified when thou speakest, and be clear when thou judgest" (verse 4). Here God is being vindicated by the cleansing and the judging of His people!

Through God's creative power, we are renewed in His image, bringing glory to Him by allowing that power to work in us. No wonder, then, that the words of the third angel focus on obedience. Following the warning of judgment, the call to glorify God, and the proclamation to worship the Creator, the third angel says, "Here is the patience of the saints: here are they that keep the commandments of God, and the faith of Jesus" (Revelation 14:12).

The people depicted in Revelation 14:12 keep the commandments (plural) of God, not just the fourth. The context places them in the time of the mark of the beast, when the world will be mired in deep apostasy. Yet despite all the disobedience around them, these "saints" don't receive the mark of the beast. They are not overcome by the prevailing evil and disobedience that sweep the world. The Lord will have a faithful church who keep His commandments though all the world be against them, and thus they will glorify Him in the full and final display of His love. Revelation 14:12 makes this point plain.

The judgment brought to view in verse 6 brings glory to God because when it is completed, heavenly beings cry out: "True and righteous are thy judgments" (Revelation 16:7). On earth, meanwhile, individuals are called to glorify God. This can be accomplished only by His creative power working in them, a power attained through "faith in Jesus" that enables them to "keep the commandments of God" and thus give glory to Him. All these elements reach their climax just before the second coming of Jesus. Thus, Revelation 14 is the culmination of the gospel as taught for centuries in the shadows and types of the sanctuary service.

In the context of the final generation who live during the close of the great antitypical day of atonement, a people with a special calling to "[perfect] holiness in the fear of God" (2 Corinthians 7:1), this statement from Ellen White has great pertinence:

> A daily and yearly typical [earthly system] atonement is no longer to be made, but the atoning sacrifice through a mediator is essential because of the constant commission of sin. Jesus is officiating in the presence of God, offering up His shed blood, as it had been a lamb slain. Jesus presents the oblation offered for every offense and every shortcoming of the sinner.[3]

Whose "constant commission of sin" makes the atoning sacrifice through a mediator "essential"? Only those whose sins are brought into the sanctuary. Only those who profess to serve the living God. Only those whose names are written in heaven. The sins of God's professed people alone still require Christ's mediation in the heavenly sanctuary because only their sins are dealt with there!

Jesus continues to minister the merits of His death. He had to die only once, but He still has to minister because of the sins of those who have claimed His sacrifice and mediation on their behalf. We keep sinning; therefore, Jesus keeps mediating, just as those who sinned in Israel constantly needed a priest mediating for them. We already have our sacrifice, finished, complete, irreversible, but we still need the mediator to apply the blood in our behalf. "He is also able to save to the uttermost those who come to God through Him, since He ever lives to make intercession for them" (Hebrews 7:25, NKJV).

We wonder why Jesus hasn't returned.

If He came now, what would happen to His people? Who would mediate for them? He's in heaven still to "make intercession" for us because we are still sinning. As long as we sin, we need a mediator. But someday, whether we are ready or not, He will return "without sin." Our sins have delayed His return, but eventually He will come anyway.

According to the book of Hebrews, Jesus will "appear the second time without sin unto salvation" (Hebrews 9:28). He will no longer be our sin-bearer, either as sacrifice or as priest. One verse in the Bible will one day no longer be true: "If any man sin, we have an advocate with the Father, Jesus Christ the righteous" (1 John 2:1). Obviously, when Jesus returns, when His high-priestly ministry is finished, we no longer will have Him as our Advo-

cate in the heavenly sanctuary.
Writes Ellen White:

Says the prophet: "Who may abide the day of His coming? and who shall stand when He appeareth? for He is like a refiner's fire, and like fuller's soap: and He shall sit as a refiner and purifier of silver: and He shall purify the sons of Levi, and purge them as gold and silver, that they may offer unto the Lord an offering in righteousness." Malachi 3:2, 3. Those who are living upon the earth when the intercession of Christ shall cease in the sanctuary above are to stand in the sight of a holy God without a mediator.[4]

Sooner or later, Jesus is going to have finished His mediation. Sooner or later, God's people will no longer have a High Priest interceding for them with the Father. Sooner or later, we are to "stand in the sight of a holy God without a mediator." What are the implications of the cessation of Christ's ministry for those who have been needing it?

Those who are living upon the earth when the intercession of Christ shall cease in the sanctuary above are to stand in the sight of a holy God without a mediator. Their robes must be spotless, their characters must be purified from sin by the blood of sprinkling. Through the grace of God and their own diligent effort they must be conquerors in the battle with evil.[5]

Wait a minute! What happened to justification by faith?

What about the cross? What about the altar of burnt of-fering that preceded the priestly mediation in the earthly tabernacle? What about forgiveness, assurance, accep-tance? How do we reconcile these words from Ellen White with these from Paul: "Being justified by faith, we have peace with God through our Lord Jesus Christ" (Ro-mans 5:11)? Or with these, "We conclude that a man is justified by faith apart from the deeds of the law" (Ro-mans 3:28, NKJV).

These questions can be asked in one, which is the crux of what ails Adventism today: How do we put to-gether Ellen White's statements about the character per-fection of the final generation with what Jesus has done on the cross?

It's easy.

---

1. *The Great Controversy,* pp. 430, 431.
2. Ibid., p. 425.
3. *Selected Messages,* bk. 1, p. 344.
4. *The Great Controversy,* p. 425.
5. Ibid.

Chapter **15**

# Faith Versus Works

**I**n recent years, the Seventh-day Adventist Church has been battered by "every wind of doctrine" (Ephesians 4:14). As a result, many church members have been blown out, while others remain but are buffeted by each new breeze that blows by. As more storms brew, Adventists don't need a weatherman to see which way the wind's blowing.

Numerous doctrinal disputes have swept, or are sweeping, the denomination. Attacks on 1844 and the investigative judgment arise with relative frequency. Questions about Ellen White, her inspiration, and her theological role continue to batter Adventism. Incessant debates continue over the 1888 General Conference in Minneapolis and what it means for the church today. The controversy over the prefall or postfall nature of Christ storms within our ranks. Adventists still wrestle over the reality of the heavenly sanctuary. Righteousness by faith has bitterly divided the church. Speculative theories about what happened and what *didn't* happen at the cross still ruffle Adventist feathers.

All these topics are relevant (even if some are more relevant than others), yet none tackles the major problem. All are important, but most are only surface manifestations of the crucial issue. These conflicts, particularly righteousness by faith, the role of Ellen White, the nature of Christ, even what happened in 1844, can be traced to one simple question: How do we relate the cross with Spirit of Prophecy statements about the character perfection of the final generation? This question is the bottom line in most theological debates going on in the Adventist Church today. How we deal with this question of character development vis-à-vis the cross affects our theology in almost every other area.

Some have accepted views of justification by faith that nullify Ellen White's statements about perfection. Others have taken views of her statements about perfection that nullify justification by faith. Both are extreme positions. One does not have to cancel the other. When properly understood, these two positions actually enhance each other.

Exacerbating the controversy are those who pile up Spirit of Prophecy quotations in order to prove their position regarding character perfection. In addition to her words from *The Great Controversy* quoted in the previous chapter, are such statements as these:

"Christ is waiting with longing desire for the manifestation of Himself in His church. When the character of Christ shall be perfectly reproduced in His people, then He will come to claim them as his own."[1]

"Are we striving with all our power to attain to the stature of men and women in Christ? Are we seeking for His fullness, ever pressing toward the mark set before us—the perfection of His character? When the Lord's people reach this mark, they will be sealed in their foreheads."[2]

"Satan could find nothing in the Son of God that would enable him to gain the victory. He had kept His Father's commandments, and there was no sin in Him that Satan could use to his advantage. This is the condition in which those must be found who shall stand in the time of trouble."[4]

"I also saw that many do not realize what they must be in order to live in the sight of the Lord without a high priest in the sanctuary through the time of trouble. Those who receive the seal of the living God and are protected in the time of trouble must reflect the image of Jesus fully."[4]

Unfortunately, those whose religion is built only on these and similar statements often neglect the following Ellen White quotes:

"We are not to be anxious about what Christ and God think of us, but about what God thinks of Christ, our Substitute. Ye are accepted in the Beloved."[5]

"Look at Moses and the prophets; look at Daniel and Joseph and Elijah. Look at these men, and find me one sentence where they ever claimed to be sinless. The very soul that is in close relation to Christ, beholding His purity and excellency, will fall before Him with shamefaced-ness."[6]

"The law demands righteousness, and this the sinner owes to the law; but he is incapable of rendering it. The only way in which he can attain to righteousness is through faith. By faith he can bring to God the merits of Christ, and the Lord places the obedience of His Son to the sinner's account. Christ's righteousness is accepted in place of man's failure, and God receives, pardons, jus-tifies, the repentant, believing soul, treats him as though he were righteous, and loves him as He loves His Son. This is how faith is accounted righteousness."[7]

"While we should realize our sinful condition, we are to rely upon Christ as our righteousness, our sanctifica-tion, and our redemption. We cannot answer the charges of Satan against us. Christ alone can make an effectual plea in our behalf. He is able to silence the accuser with arguments founded not upon our merits, but on His own."[8]

This tension regarding faith and works exists, not only in Ellen White, but in Scripture. Genesis says that Cain "brought an offering of the fruit of the ground" (Genesis 4:3, NKJV), an offering of works that God rejected; Abel offered to God from the "firstlings of his flock" (verse 4), an offer made in faith, which God accepted. Later, though, God declared, "I desired mercy, and not sacri-fice; and the knowledge of God more than burnt offer-ings" (Hosea 6:6).

Paul said, "If Abraham were justified by works, he hath whereof to glory; but not before God" (Romans 4:2). Yet James asked, "Was not Abraham our father justified by works, when he had offered Isaac his son upon the altar?" (James 2:21). Paul again writes: "We conclude that a man is justified by faith apart from the deeds of the law" (Romans 3:28, NKJV). Yet John in the book of Revelation writes: "Blessed are those who do His commandments, that they may have the right to the tree of life, and may enter through the gates into the city" (Revelation 22:14, NKJV).

Jesus Himself said to the woman caught in adultery: "Neither do I condemn you; go and sin no more" (John 8:11, NKJV); yet on another occasion Jesus said, "If your right eye causes you to sin, pluck it out and cast it from you; for it is more profitable for you that one of your members perish, than for your whole body to be cast into hell" (Matthew 5:29, NKJV).

These statements, either in the Spirit of Prophecy or in the Bible, don't contradict each other. Instead, the question is: How do we balance them? The place that reveals that true balance, as we will see in the next chapter, is the sanctuary.

---

1. *Christ's Object Lessons,* p. 69.
2. *Our High Calling,* p. 150.
3. *The Great Controversy,* p. 623.
4. *Early Writings,* p. 71.
5. *Selected Messages,* bk. 2, pp. 32, 33.
6. Ibid., bk. 3, p. 353.
7. Ibid., bk. 1, p. 367.
8. *Testimonies for the Church,* vol. 5, p. 472.

# Chapter 16

# When Your Name Comes Up

The first lesson about balance taught in the sanctuary service deals with the sacrifice of the animal, a symbol of Jesus on the cross. Here is the foundation upon which the entire plan of salvation rests. Only in the context of the cross can we understand the sanctuary service, particularly the investigative judgment. Without the cross, the sanctuary service and the investigative judgment become legalistic and antigospel.

What does the cross mean for those whose names will appear in the judgment? What has the cross done for those who will live without a mediator? These are crucial questions, and the right understanding of the answers can make the difference between eternal life or eternal destruction.

A sinner in ancient Israel brought his sacrifice to the sanctuary because he had committed a sin. He sinned because he was a sinner. He was a sinner because he was born that way, alienated and separated from God. It is the same with us. We come to Jesus because we have sinned, and we sin because we are sinners.

Originally man was not an estranged and alienated sinner. "God created man in His own image; in the image of God He created him; male and female He created them" (Genesis 1:27, NKJV). In the beginning, God created man in His own moral likeness. Adam was not naturally a sinner, not innately alienated from God, as we are today. Only after he and Eve sinned did the estrangement start: "They heard the sound of the Lord God walking in the garden in the cool of the day, and Adam and his wife hid themselves from the presence of the Lord God among the trees of the garden" (Genesis 3:8, NKJV).

After Adam sinned, his children, instead of being made in the image of God, were fashioned in the image of Adam himself, now a sinner. "Adam lived an hundred and thirty years, and begat a son in his own likeness, after his image" (Genesis 5:3). Coiled deep within Adam's loins, we all were corrupted because of his sin. Like a drug addict who spawns a child of warped limbs, we are our father's deformed children, cursed with spiritual birth defects that have alienated us from our Maker. "You, who once were alienated and enemies in your mind by wicked works, yet now He has reconciled in the body of His flesh through death, to present you holy, and blameless, and irreproachable in His sight" (Colossians 1:21, 22).

Modern psychology rejects this idea of man's inherent evil nature, claiming that it overburdens us with a destructive sense of shame and guilt. Modern psychology teaches that man is innately good, that human nature is basically moral. It's true that selfless acts of morality and kindness have been recorded throughout history, but they are usually manifest amid the backdrop of a greater, overwhelming evil. While millions of men, women, and children were being gassed, shot, and burned in Europe by the Nazis, the scattered souls who risked their lives to try and save them don't negate the rule. On the contrary, they're the exceptions who prove it. In the context of the savage pages of human history, to say that "all have sinned, and come short of the glory of God" (Romans 3:23) is almost an understatement.

Colossians 1:21, 22, however, talks about Jesus, who has "reconciled" us to God "in the body of His flesh through death." Jesus died in order to save us from the destruction and misery caused by sin. How?

In a theological sense, the Bible teaches that there have been only two men—Adam and Jesus. As the natural children of Adam, we have been legally condemned because of his sin. We are not guilty of Adam's specific sin, but we have suffered the results of it. By nature, we are sinners because of the legacy passed on to us by our father Adam.

A man robs a bank and then flees. While a fugitive, he sires children. For years, these children, like their father, live an underground life, hiding, lying, stealing, committing crime. They have suffered the results of their father's initial transgression, as seen in the corrupt life that they have lived because of it. Eventually, the family is apprehended by the police. Those children are placed in reform school, not for their father's bank robbery, but for their own crimes, which came about as a result of the father's.

This situation is analogous to our condition. Because of his transgression, Adam fled from God. As his natural offspring, we have been fleeing ever since, with 6,000 years of misery as the result. We are not guilty of Adam's sin any more than the children of the bank robber are guilty of his. But like those children, we have been corrupted by our father's sin. "Through one man [Adam] sin entered the world, and death through sin, and thus death spread to all men, because all sinned" (Romans 5:12, NKJV). Adam brought sin, and sin brought death. Therefore, because all sin, all die.

Suppose, however, someone offers to legally adopt the bank robber's children and turn them from a life of crime. This, in a weak sense, is what God has done for us in Jesus. Jesus came as the new father of the race, the new legal head of humanity, adopting from Adam all the children who will receive Him. "When the fullness of the time had come, God sent forth His Son, born of woman, born under the law, to redeem those who were under the law, that we might receive the adoption as sons. And because you are sons, God has sent forth the Spirit of His Son into your hearts, crying out, Abba, Father" (Galatians 4:4-6, NKJV).[1]

As were the children of that bank robber, we have all been born into a corrupted and condemned family, alienated and estranged from God. From Adam we have received a sinful nature. Jesus wants to adopt us and bring us into His own family. "For this reason I bow my knees to the Father of our Lord Jesus Christ, from whom the whole family in heaven and earth is named" (Ephesians 3:14, 15, NKJV).

Paul writes:

> "As through one man's offense [Adam's] judgment came to all men, resulting in condemnation, even so through one Man's righteous act [Jesus'] the free gift came to all men, resulting in justification of life. For as by one man's disobedience [Adam's] many were made sinners, so also by one Man's obedience [Jesus'] many will be made righteous" (Romans 5:18, 19, NKJV).

Adoption in the earthly sense, however, doesn't fully explain what Christ has accomplished for us. If one of the bank robber's children committed murder, it would take more than adoption to save him. Jesus did more than just adopt us. He justified us as well (see Romans 5:1).

Justification entails the legal declaration of forgiveness. It is the gift of a perfectly righteous, sinless, and holy character credited to us even though we can never possess it ourselves. We can reflect it, even reflect it "perfectly," but we can never equal it.

> Our Lord and Saviour laid aside His dominion, His riches and glory, and sought after us, that He might save us from misery and make us like Himself. He humbled Himself and took our nature that

145

we might be able to learn of Him and, imitating His life of benevolence and self-denial, follow Him step by step to heaven. You cannot equal the copy; but you can resemble it and, according to your ability, do likewise.[2]

Our dilemma remains, however, because God accepts only perfect righteousness, not even a perfect reflection or resemblance of it. Because of Adam's sin and the corruption it wrought in humankind, none of us has ever been capable of producing a perfect character. If left to ourselves, we would perish, without hope, without God, dead in trespasses and sin. Yet, precisely because we are so helpless, so utterly incapable of saving ourselves, Jesus came, worked out that perfect righteousness in His own life, and offers to credit it to us freely.

Imagine a school that gave only two grades for each course—either pass or fail. But in order to pass, the student must have a 100 percent average. A 95 percent earns the same failing grade as a 20 percent. The student must have a perfect score on every paper, quiz, or exam; otherwise, he fails. If he makes one mistake, ever answers one question wrong, he fails.

The same with redemption. No matter who we are, how healthy our genes, how proper our upbringing, we all have sinned, and therefore can never achieve within ourselves the perfect 100 percent righteousness needed to be redeemed. Even if we were to *become* perfect, never sinning again, we could not produce the righteousness needed for salvation because of our past sins. No matter how hard we try, how hard we pray, how converted and sanctified we ever become, unless we have a perfect righteousness *credited to us,* outside of us, we are lost souls. Therefore, all our righteousness and good works, even those done under the inspiration of the Holy Spirit, can no more save us than can all the washing, scrubbing, and manicures make a pig kosher.

But Jesus, because of His perfect life, has that perfect righteousness, that 100 percent score. He stands as the new Head of humanity, so that, *in Him,* we have that perfect life as our own. It's as if in that school the teacher were to say, "Believe in me, and when the day comes to average your grades, no matter what they are, I will blot them all out, and you can have my 100 percent instead of your failing marks." The righteousness of Jesus Christ, which He wrought out for us, independently of us, He freely offers us in place of our own filthy garments. "I will clothe thee," Jesus says, "with change of raiment" (Zechariah 3:4).

This is the essence of the gospel, the good news. No matter who we are or what we've done, Jesus Christ can forgive everything and allow us to stand in the sight of God as perfect and as accepted by the Father as He was, because He will freely credit to us, as undeserving as we are, His perfect righteousness. We are then no longer sinners deserving death, but true sons and daughters of God, as was Adam before he fell. We don't have to earn it; we don't have to reach a standard to attain it; we don't have to come up to a level to be granted it. We don't have to reach 70 percent or 90 percent before the covering will be given us, which then makes up the difference. On the contrary, like a garment woven in the loom of heaven, Christ's righteousness will cover us completely from wherever we start. That 100 percent is immediately granted to the converted soul no matter his grade point average. And it stays with him always—though not unconditionally, as we will see in the next chapter.

> The great work that is wrought for the sinner who is spotted and stained by evil is the work of justification. By Him who speaketh truth he is declared righteous. The Lord imputes unto the believer the righteousness of Christ and pronounces him righteous before the universe. He transfers his sins to Jesus, the sinner's representative, substitute, and surety. Upon Christ He lays the iniquity of every soul that believeth. "He hath made him to be sin for us, who knew no sin; that we might be made the righteousness of God in him" (2 Corinthians 5:21).[3]

"We conclude that a man is justified by faith apart from the deeds of the law" (Romans 3:28, NKJV).

The good news gets even better! This covering of Christ's perfect righteousness (called *forensic justification* by theologians) covers us in the investigative judgment when our names come up. That's the most important purpose of justification! What good would justification be if in the judgment, when we need it the most, it were no longer valid?

Some believe that we are initially justified by Christ's righteousness, but that in the judgment, because we are judged by works, our final justification comes by the attainment of character perfection through grace. That would be as if in that school, the 100 percent credited to you were removed the day the grades were averaged, and you were then expected to stand in your own works. (Even if you have been making 100 percent on all your exams the last few weeks, your past grades would still flunk you!) In the book of Galatians, Paul warns against this type of thinking: "I do not set aside the grace of God; for if righteousness comes through the law, then Christ died in vain" (Galatians 2:21, NKJV). He then writes, "Are you so foolish? Having begun in the Spirit, are you now being made perfect by the flesh?" (Galatians 3:3, NKJV). He warns too: "You have become estranged from Christ, you who attempt to be justified by law; you have fallen from grace. For we through the Spirit eagerly wait for the hope or righteousness by faith" (Galatians 5:4, 5, NKJV).

The sanctuary teaches the truth of righteousness in Christ alone. Every animal sacrificed in the Jewish economy symbolized the death of Jesus, whose righteousness alone could bring salvation to mankind. "It is not possible that the blood of bulls and goats could take away sins" (Hebrews 10:4, NKJV). Those sacrifices pointed forward to Jesus on the cross, the only source of redemption.

Every morning and evening, a special sacrifice was made in Israel, a burnt offering that symbolized the continual availability of Christ's righteousness for the sinner. It was called the daily, or the regular, "continual burnt offering." "This is what you shall offer on the altar: two lambs of the first year, day by day continually. One lamb you shall offer in the morning, and the other lamb you shall offer at twilight. . . . This shall be a continual burnt offering throughout your generations at the door of the tabernacle of meeting before the Lord" (Exodus 29:38-42, NKJV).

This continual burnt sacrifice assured the penitent Israelite of the constant availability of forgiveness. If he were sick or away from Jerusalem or for some reason couldn't get to the sanctuary, he could still reach out by faith to the promise symbolized by this continual sacrifice, which burned on the altar twenty-four hours a day, every day, all year long—even on the Day of Atonement.

This point is crucial. During the solemn ceremony of Yom Kippur, the daily morning and evening sacrifice was burning. All through the service, this burnt offering, symbolic of Christ's death in our behalf, was burning on the altar (see Numbers 29:7-11).

All through the Day of Atonement, the merits of Christ's righteousness, symbolized by "the regular burnt offering," covered the sinner, even while the priest was taking out all the sins from the Most Holy Place and the people were to be "clean from all your sins before the Lord" (Leviticus 16:30, NKJV).

What, then, happens to us on the Day of Atonement? What is the process that takes place in the investigative judgment? Balancing the perspective of animal sacrifice with the second apartment service, what happens to those written in the book of life when their names come up in judgment?

"As the books of record are opened in the judgment," Ellen White writes, "the lives of all who have believed on Jesus come in review."[4] Only those who have believed on

Jesus are dealt with in this judgment, just as in the Day of Atonement ritual, only those sins that had been brought into the sanctuary were blotted out—the sins of the penitent believer.

Christ's work in the heavenly sanctuary is depicted in the third chapter of Zechariah, which has "Joshua the high priest standing before the Angel of the Lord, and Satan standing at his right hand to oppose him" (Zechariah 3:1, NKJV). The vision shows Joshua "clothed with filthy garments" (verse 3), symbolizing the spiritual condition of God's true people, while Satan accuses him before the Angel of the Lord.

Joshua, Ellen White writes, "cannot defend himself or his people from Satan's accusations. He does not claim that Israel are free from fault. In his filthy garments, symbolizing the sins of the people, which he bears as their representative, he stands before the Angel, confessing their guilt, yet pointing to their repentance and humiliation, relying upon the mercy of a sin-pardoning Redeemer and in faith claiming the promises of God."[6]

The Angel of the Lord, who is "Christ Himself, the Saviour of sinners,"[7] then silences Satan, the accuser of the brethren. " 'The Lord rebuke you, Satan! The Lord who has chosen Jerusalem rebuke you! Is this not a brand plucked from the fire?' " (Zechariah 3:2, NKJV). The Lord, rejecting Satan's accusations, then says to Joshua, " 'See, I have removed your iniquity from you, and I will clothe you with rich robes' " (verse 4, NKJV). Then they "put a clean turban on his head, and they put the clothes on him" (verse 5, NKJV).

Ellen White continues: "His own [Joshua's] sins and those of his people were pardoned. Israel were clothed with 'change of raiment'—the righteousness of Christ imputed to them."[8]

Satan, as he accused Joshua, accuses all the followers of Christ in every age.[9]·

Man cannot meet these charges himself. In his sin-stained garments, confessing his guilt, he stands before God. But Jesus our Advocate presents an effectual plea in behalf of all who by repentance and faith have committed the keeping of their souls to Him. He pleads their cause and vanquishes their accuser by the mighty arguments of Calvary. His perfect obedience to God's law, even unto the death of the cross, has given Him all power in heaven and in earth, and He claims of His Father mercy and reconciliation for guilty man.[10]

The good news is that what Christ did here for Joshua is what He does for His faithful followers in the investigative judgment! He presents *His* righteousness, *His* worthiness, *His* perfect 100 percent in our stead when our names come up.

All who have truly repented of sin, and by faith claimed the blood of Christ as their atoning sacrifice, have had pardon entered against their names in the books of heaven; as they have become partakers of the righteousness of Christ, and their characters are found in harmony with the law of God, their sins will be blotted out, and they themselves will be accounted worthy of eternal life.[11]

While Jesus is pleading for the subjects of His grace, Satan accuses them before God as transgressors. . . . He points to the defects of character, the unlikeness to Christ, which has dishonored their Redeemer, to all the sins that he has tempted them to commit, and because of these he claims them as his subjects.

Jesus does not excuse their sins, but shows their penitence and faith, and, claiming for them forgiveness, He lifts His wounded hands before the Father and the holy angels, saying: I know them by name. I have graven them on the palms of My hands.[12]

Ellen White, despite her strong emphasis on the character perfection of the final generation, never teaches that our characters justify us in the judgment. Character development can never justify! Ellen White always points to the work of the cross, the blood of Jesus, carrying the penitent sinner all the way through the investigative judgment. Nothing else will work, for we all stand condemned before those two tablets of stone in the Most Holy Place.

What about her statements regarding those who live without a mediator once Christ's work is finished in the heavenly sanctuary? Are these people sinners? Of course. Have they ever broken God's law? Of course. Have they, therefore, any righteousness in and of themselves that can get them through the judgment? Of course not. What saves them in the judgment, then, is exactly what saves all Christ's faithful followers: Jesus lifting His wounded hands before the Father and saying: "I have graven them upon the palms of My hands." The final generation is saved the same way every other generation is saved—by the righteousness of Christ imputed to them.

No question, this final generation will be a special people. They will have a unique sanctification experience; they will be a people who will never die, a people who will be translated and who will honor and glorify God in the climax of the great controversy by keeping all His commandments though the world be arrayed against them. Yet this experience is not what saves them! No matter what their experience in holiness is, even if they haven't sinned in twenty years, they still have past sins that would condemn them in the judgment if not for the covering of Christ's perfect righteousness credited to them.

"Those who are living upon the earth when the intercession of Christ shall cease in the sanctuary above are to stand in the sight of a holy God without a mediator. Their robes must be spotless, their characters . . . purified from sin by the blood of sprinkling."[13]

Look at the time element here. The names of these individuals must have already come up in the judgment because Christ's work *is finished*. His intercession in the sanctuary has ceased. By this time their sins have already been blotted out in the same way that the sins of every generation have been dealt with—Jesus standing before the Father and pleading His own righteousness in their behalf.

It's over. They have already been sealed. Their character perfection is not what carried them through the judgment; it is what they have become and are. These people are going to live after the judgment is over and probation is closed. " 'He who is unjust, let him be unjust still; he who is filthy, let him be filthy still; he who is righteous, let him be righteous still; he who is holy, let him be holy still' " (Revelation 22:11, NKJV).

These people will be living, literally, at the end of the world. Everything collapses around them as the planet degenerates into "a time of trouble such as never was." This final generation will have lost every material possession. They will face hunger, privation, weariness, and persecution. Fleeing for their lives, these people—hungry, tired, fearful, their only hope in the Lord—won't be thinking about sleeping with their neighbor's spouse or anything like that. Their situation will be desperate. They will have to cling so closely to the Lord that they wouldn't dare do anything which would separate them from their only refuge and source of strength.

Some discard character perfection because they think that it nullifies the gospel, while others nullify the gospel because they think character perfection saves them. Both sides are wrong. The Lord Jesus is going to perfect the characters of a final generation in a grand and glorious climax of the great controversy that will display to the universe what God has been saying all along: His law *can* be kept. Yet this final generation is justified only by what Jesus Christ has accomplished for them, outside of them, 2,000 years ago at Calvary. Anything else is salvation by works. Indeed, far from nullifying the cross, the investigative judgment brings it to its climax.

Of course, not everyone saved will be part of this final generation. Many alive now will not be alive when Jesus returns. They will rest in their graves and then rise in the first resurrection with the righteous of all generations from Adam on. They will not have the experience of the 144,000. Some Adventists, therefore, have been tempted to think, "Well, I won't worry about being part of this last group, anyway. If I can be part of the first resurrection only, that's fine."

We're such ungrateful, pernicious buffoons. It's a wonder Christ didn't leave us to die in our sins. Jesus has done so much for us, accomplished so much in our behalf, has promised so much to us, and yet we want to return as little as possible. Ellen White wrote: "I want not only to be pardoned for the transgression of God's holy law, but I want to be lifted into the sunshine of God's countenance. Not simply to be admitted to heaven, but to have an abundant entrance."[14]

Because there will be people saved who haven't had the sanctification experience of the 144,000, some wonder why they should even try to be in this final group that will be completely victorious over sin. Who wants the hassle of giving glory to God in the climax of the ages? Who wants to be alive when Jesus comes? Who wants never to die but be translated? Those who don't—won't. With such an attitude, they will rise in a resurrection, but not necessarily the first one!

Besides the righteousness of Christ that covers the sinner, symbolized by the continual burnt offering, there is another aspect of the judgment—those tablets of stone in the second apartment of the sanctuary. These represent the law of God, the standard by which we are judged. Make no mistake, those who have their names written in the book of life are judged by their works: "Judgment must begin at the house of God: and if it first begins at us, what shall the end be of them that obey not the gospel of God?" (1 Peter 4:17). Make no mistake, either—names written in the book of life can be blotted out during that judgment: "He that overcometh, the same shall be clothed in white raiment; and I will not blot out his name out of the book of life, but I will confess his name before my Father, and before his angels" (Revelation 3:5).

Names stay, names go. What determines which?

---

1. See also Romans 8:15 and Ephesians 1:5.

2. *Testimonies for the Church,* vol. 2, p. 170.

3. *Selected Messages,* bk. 1, p. 392.

4. *The Great Controversy,* p. 483.

5. *The Great Controversy,* p. 480; other statements about the ones coming up in the investigative judgment are: "All who have ever entered the service of God" (GC); "all who have ever taken upon themselves the name of Christ"; "the lives of all His [God's] professed believers" (*Christ's Object Lessons,* p. 310).

6. *Testimonies for the Church,* vol. 5, pp. 468, 469.

7. Ibid., p. 469.

8. Ibid.

9. See Ibid., p. 470.

10. Ibid., p. 471.

11. *The Great Controversy,* p. 483.

12. Ibid., p. 484.

13. Ibid., p. 425.

14. *Selected Messages,* bk. 2, p. 381.

# 17

# The Judas in All of Us

Not only does Christ cover us with His righteousness the moment we truly accept Him, but that covering will remain with us through the investigative judgment. *His* obedience to the law of God, *His* perfection, *His* merits allow us to stand perfect in the sight of God when our name comes up in the great antitypical Day of Atonement. That's good news.

Yet it gets even better. Jesus will never forsake us for our sins. The God who stepped out of eternity into humanity, who left the glory of heaven for a crown of thorns on earth, will not abandon us because of our sins. He came to die for them, instead.

"God commendeth his love toward us, in that, while

we were yet sinners, Christ died for us" (Romans 5:8).

"Surely he hath borne our griefs, and carried our sorrows; yet we did esteem him stricken, smitten of God, and afflicted. But he was wounded for our transgressions, he was bruised for our iniquities; the chastisement of our peace was upon him; and with his stripes we are healed" (Isaiah 53:4, 5).

Christ wasn't obliged to die for us. The earth could have been cast off with less effect on the universe than the demise of a single cell has on the human body. Yet Jesus came to redeem this planet anyway, and the love that promoted this act will not forsake us because of our sin.

But doesn't Jesus say that it is better to have our eyes plucked out or our hands cut off rather than to burn in hell? What about His words: " 'Many will say to Me in that day, "Lord, Lord, have we not prophesied in Your name, cast out demons in Your name, and done many wonders in Your name?" And then I will declare to them, "I never knew you; depart from Me." ' " (Matthew 7:22, 23, NKJV). What about Paul's warning: "I keep under my body, and bring it into subjection: lest that by any means, when I have preached to others, I myself should be a castaway" (1 Corinthians 9:27). What about all the Old Testament omens of doom, destruction, and judgment if Israel refused to repent and reform? What about the judgments that fell upon the nation because of its sin?

I repeat: Jesus will never forsake us because of our sins. *He won't forsake us because of our sins—but we may forsake Jesus for them!* A name is blotted out of the book of life because that person has chosen sin over Christ. The blotting out of the name is God simply respecting the choice that the person has already made.

The Feast of Unleavened Bread drew near, which is called Passover. And the chief priests and the scribes sought how they might kill Him [Jesus], for they feared the people. Then Satan entered Judas, surnamed Iscariot, who was numbered among the twelve. So he went his way and conferred with the chief priests and captains, how he might betray Him to them. And they were glad, and agreed to give him money. Then he promised and sought opportunity to betray Him to them in the absence of the multitude (Luke 22:1-6, NKJV).

Who forsook whom? Did Jesus desert Judas because of his sin? No, Judas forsook Jesus, and his ruin is a dramatic example of what causes names to be taken out of the book of life.

"Then Satan entered Judas, surnamed Iscariot, who was numbered among the twelve" (verse 3, NKJV). Why did he enter Judas and not John, James, or Peter? Satan wanted them all. Jesus even warned Peter in that same chapter: "Simon, Simon! Indeed, Satan has asked for you, that he may sift you as wheat" (Luke 22:31, NKJV).

Why Judas? After all, he had an experience with Jesus. He had been stirred by the miracles of the Saviour. He saw the lame, the blind, the sick brought to Christ's feet and healed by a word or a touch. He saw Him raise the dead, cast out demons, and multiply the fish and the loaves. "He recognized the teaching of Christ as superior to all that he had ever heard. He loved the Great Teacher, and desired to be with Him. He felt a desire to be changed in character and life, and he hoped to experience this through connecting himself with Jesus."[1]

Haven't all Christ's followers through the ages experienced something of the same? Have they not all not loved Jesus and desired to be with Him? Have they not been impressed by the miracles that Christ performed? Have they not recognized His teaching as superior to anything else they have heard, and have they not, like Judas, felt a desire "to be changed in character and life"? Indeed, is there not a little Judas in all of us?

Obviously, the Holy Spirit had touched Judas. Perhaps, for that reason, Jesus "gave him a place among the twelve. He trusted him to do the work of an evangelist. He endowed him with power to heal the sick and to cast out devils."[2] Judas was not merely accepted by Christ, he was among His inner circle of twelve, even given supernatural powers. Judas could have become the most powerful disciple of them all, perhaps even writing a book of the Bible: the Gospel of St. Judas. If anyone had the opportunity to be saved by Jesus, it was Judas.

Jesus told His followers: " 'Behold, I give you the authority to trample on serpents and scorpions, and over all the power of the enemy, and nothing shall by any means hurt you. Nevertheless do not rejoice in this, that the spirits are subject to you, but rather rejoice because your names are written in heaven' " (Luke 10:19, 20). If "the lives of all His [God's] professed believers"[3] are written in the book of life—then surely the name of Judas Iscariot must have been written there.

What, then, happened?

Ellen White tells us clearly. "Judas did not come to the point of surrendering himself fully to Christ. He did not give up his worldly ambition or his love of money. While he accepted the position of a minister of Christ, he did not bring himself under the divine molding."[4]

What was the result?

"He had fostered the evil spirit of avarice until it had become the ruling motive of his life. The love of mammon overbalanced his love for Christ. Through becoming the slave of one vice he gave himself to Satan, to be driven to any lengths in sin."[5]

Judas indulged in one main sin, and it brought his ruin, not because Jesus couldn't forgive it, but because Judas didn't accept that forgiveness. Refusing to repent, he literally chose that sin over Jesus—an example of what happens to all who, though written in the book of life, are eventually blotted out of it.

Satan knows the gospel. Satan understands righteousness by faith better than any Seventh-day Adventist. He believes in the cross. After all, he was there! He knows that "there is therefore now no condemnation to them which are in Christ Jesus" (Romans 8:1). He comprehends that "the gift of God is eternal life through Jesus Christ our Lord" (Romans 6:23). He knows that "a man is not justified by the works of the law, but by the faith of Jesus Christ" (Galatians 2:16).

Satan realizes, too, that nothing he can do will nullify or reverse what Jesus has done at the cross. He understands that no matter who we are or what we have done, we can find complete pardon and restoration in Jesus. He knows God's great love for us, and that neither "height nor depth, nor any other created thing, shall be able to separate us from the love of God which is in Christ Jesus" (Romans 8:39, NKJV). Because he understands all these things, he knows that Jesus will never forsake us.

Therefore he tries to get us to forsake Jesus instead, and the only way he can do this is to lead us into sin and then keep us in it. He knows if he can do that, we will ultimately choose that sin over Jesus—just as Judas did.

"Then Satan entered into Judas." Why Judas? Because, as Ellen White wrote, "he gave himself to Satan." And the reason he gave himself to Satan was because he had indulged in a sin that became the ruling power of his life.

Jesus did not abandon Judas. To the end, Jesus sought to save him.

Judas was not yet wholly hardened. Even after he had twice pledged himself to betray the Saviour, there was opportunity for repentance. At the Passover supper Jesus proved His divinity by revealing the traitor's purpose. He tenderly included Judas in the ministry to the disciples. But the last appeal of love was unheeded. Then the case of Judas was decided, and the feet that Jesus had washed went forth to the betrayer's work.[6]

So hardened was Judas that even with Jesus before him in the flesh, Judas chose his sin over the Saviour. If Judas could reject Jesus even after the Saviour washed his feet, Christians today must recognize how easy it is to choose sin over the Saviour.

For this reason, the battle with sin is central to the fight of faith for those who will ultimately stand on the sea of glass. We must get victory over sin, or it will get victory over us. We must overcome, or be overcome. Sin is deadly, not because it can't be pardoned. God longs to pardon our sin. The cross proves that. Sin is deadly because, while it won't push God away from us, it will push us away from God. Sin separates us from God.

Who came looking for whom in Eden? God came looking for Adam and Eve. And what did they do when they heard His "voice in the garden" (Genesis 3:10)? They fled. Sin, in a more subtle way, makes us do the same.

Yet connected with Christ, Christians have the victory over sin. "There hath no temptation taken you but such as is common to man: but God is faithful, who will not suffer you to be tempted above that ye are able; but will with the temptation also make a way to escape, that ye may be able to bear it" (1 Corinthians 10:13). Is God able to make a way of escape for us or not? This verse says yes.

"The Lord knoweth how to deliver the godly out of temptations" (2 Peter 2:9). Does the Lord know how to deliver us out of temptation or not? According to this verse, He does.

"Unto him that is able to keep you from falling, and to present you faultless before the presence of his glory" (Jude 24). Is God able to keep us from falling or not? This verse says yes.

What, then, is our problem? Why are we not only still sinning, but justifying our sins by asserting that we can't overcome them or that God's law can't be kept? "We can overcome. Yes; fully, entirely. Jesus died to make a way of escape for us, that we might overcome every fault, resist every temptation, and sit down at last with Him in His throne."[7]

In the Sermon on the Mount, Jesus said, "Resist not evil: but whosoever shall smite thee on thy right cheek, turn to him the other also" (Matthew 5:39). Look at the level of morality Jesus has called us to! We think we've been great Christians if we don't retaliate when abused, yet Jesus wants to take us further, ordering us to give the abuser our other cheek.

"Whoever compels you to go one mile, go with him two" (Matthew 5:41, NKJV). We think we're such good Christians if someone asks us to do something and we do it. Yet Jesus is asking us to do more.

"Love your enemies" (Matthew 5:44). We think we've arrived when we are at peace with our enemies, or we even allow them to run over us. Yet that's not good enough. Jesus orders us to love them!

All of His words here deal with personal relationships, as do the last six commandments: "Thou shalt not bear false witness, thou shalt not kill, thou shalt not steal . . ." Jesus asks us to go beyond simply keeping the commandment that forbids adultery. He tells us not even to lust in our hearts. He asks us not simply to obey the law against murder; He tells us not even to be angry!

In the Sermon on the Mount, Jesus barely even addressed the "thou shalt nots," as if the "thou shalt nots" are axiomatic, already understood and accepted. He holds up before His followers something far deeper than a mere outward compliance with the Ten Commandments. Yet the Adventist Church is suffused with the teaching that we can't obey even the "thou shalt nots." We are told that it is impossible to keep the Ten Commandments. We are told that we will always be sinning, and that those who teach otherwise are legalists or radical perfectionists. We are told all these things, and it is called the gospel! Or called an even more ridiculous appellation: righteousness by faith! What is righteous about the idea that we must go on sinning? It's as if Jesus wants us to get a Ph.D., while those who say we can't keep the law would keep us in kindergarten!

"My little children, of whom I travail in birth again until Christ be formed in you" (Galatians 4:19).

"Always bearing about in the body the dying of the Lord Jesus, that the life also of Jesus might be made manifest in our body. For we which live are alway delivered unto death for Jesus' sake, that the life also of Jesus might be made manifest in our mortal flesh" (2 Corinthians 4:10, 11).

"I am crucified with Christ: nevertheless I live; yet not I, but Christ liveth in me" (Galatians 2:20).

Christ's life is to be "made manifest in us," a life that soared far beyond the simple "thou shalt nots" of the law. Yet some Seventh-day Adventists assert that we can't even keep the Ten Commandments.

"Christ lived a life of perfect obedience to God's law, and in this He set an example for every human being. The life that He lived in this world we are to live through His power and under His instruction."[8]

The teaching that even converted Christians can't keep God's law, or stop sinning, devastates the three angels' messages, makes a mockery of the cross, and leads to ruin.

The real issue in the great controversy, the starting point of Satan's rebellion, concerned the law of God. Satan rebelled against the law, asserting that it was unfair, unjust, and couldn't be kept. Therefore, his unwavering goal has been to cause men to break that law and thus prove his point.

From the very beginning of the great controversy

in heaven it has been Satan's purpose to overthrow the law of God. It was to accomplish this that he entered upon his rebellion against the Creator, and though he was cast out of heaven he has continued the same warfare upon the earth. To deceive men, and thus lead them to transgress God's law, is the object which he has steadfastly pursued. Whether this be accomplished by casting aside the law altogether, or by rejecting one of its precepts, the result ultimately will be the same.[9]

Ellen White could have added that Satan's objective may be reached also by teaching that the law really can't be kept. Not much difference exists between the belief that we don't have to keep the law or that we can't keep it. Either way, we will break that law, and Satan's purposes will have been accomplished.

Those who claim that we can't overcome sin really claim that we can't obey the Ten Commandments. Therefore, when Seventh-day Adventists, who have been called out with the special purpose of proclaiming God's law, assert that we can't keep it, they are nullifying the very law they have been called to uphold! How ridiculous to advocate a standard that the standard bearers themselves reject either by word or deed. If the law can't be kept, then what does the third angel mean in Revelation 14:12—"Here is the patience of the saints; here are those who keep the commandments of God and the faith of Jesus"? (NKJV).

It's eerie to hear Seventh-day Adventists reiterate the exact lie that Satan first promulgated even before the world began: that God's law can't be kept. The devil must be ecstatic. The people raised up to help disprove his lies are promoting them instead.

Why, too, would God make a law that couldn't be kept and then cast billions into the lake of fire for not keeping it? How can the standard of judgment be the Ten Commandments if they were too high to begin with? What kind of teacher gives an exam that no student can possibly pass and then flunks them all?

Most important, if men are condemned because they have broken a law that couldn't be obeyed, what's so important about Calvary? What great sacrifice did Jesus make? If we are damned by an unattainable standard to begin with, and if sin is the transgression of that standard, then sin is really God's fault. Jesus *owed* it to us to die on the cross. If sin was His fault, Calvary was the least He could do.

Both the Bible and the Spirit of Prophecy teach, however, that we can overcome, we do overcome, and that the law is the standard by which we are to live and be judged. Just because some have taught the gospel in a legalist manner is no reason to throw out the law.

The key is to balance law and grace. We must keep the distinction between what Christ has done for us at the cross—justification—and what He wants to do in us—sanctification. They are different aspects of the same gospel, with different functions. Problems arise, however, when they are separated in terms of the daily life of the believer. One without the other emasculates the gospel. If justified, we will become sanctified. Salvation does not end with the legal declaration of forgiveness any more than baptism ends with immersion. After being submerged, we must rise out of the water "in newness of life" (Romans 6:4). Redemption begins, not ends, with forgiveness, just as baptism begins, not ends, with immersion. Beware of those who want to place you under the water and leave you there!

The sanctuary teaches that salvation didn't end at Calvary because redemption does not end with forgiveness. The gospel is not just pardon, which is its foundation, but also restoration, which is its pinnacle. Justification, what Christ has done for us at the cross, cannot be separated from the law.

"Knowing that a man is not justified by the works of the law, but by the faith of Jesus Christ, even we have believed in Jesus Christ that we might be justified by the faith of Christ, and not by the works of the law" (Galatians 2:16). Here is justification, pure and simple. Here is what happened at the altar of burnt offering and the first apartment of the sanctuary. Here is the life and death of Christ for us. Yet what does the next verse say? "But if, while we seek to be justified by Christ, we ourselves also are found sinners, is therefore Christ the minister of sin? God forbid" (verse 17).

Here, in the same breath as justification, Paul warns against those who use it as an excuse for sin. Those who teach that the law can't be kept are, however subtly, giving us excuses to sin!

"We conclude that a man is justified by faith without the deeds of the law" (Romans 3:28). This is the greatest truth of the Bible. Yet a few verses later, Paul says, "Do we then make void the law through faith? God forbid: Yea, we establish the law" (verse 31).

Faith and works are inseparably linked. "As the body without the spirit is dead, so faith without works is dead also" (James 2:26).

If God's law can be kept, and He has promised His people power to keep it, why do we continue to break that law? Why do we continue to sin? If God asks His people not to sin ("Shall we continue in sin, that grace may abound? God forbid" [Romans 6:1, 2]); if God even warns that sin can destroy them ("Do not be deceived. Neither fornicators, nor idolaters, nor adulterers, nor homosexuals, nor sodomites, nor thieves, nor covetous, nor drunkards, nor revilers, nor extortioners will inherit the kingdom of God" [1 Corinthians 6:9, 10, NKJV]; and if God even promises them power not to sin ("Unto him that is able to keep you from falling" [Jude 24])—yet they continue to transgress anyway, it is only because they are *choosing* to sin.

This side of the second coming, we will always have a sinful and evil nature. We will always have to struggle with the clamors of our own fallen flesh. We will always be aware of the sin that dwells within us. This side of the second coming we will always be sinners, but we don't always have to sin! The act of sinning itself, for a converted Christian, is a conscious choice. How could it be anything else? If God promises us power not to sin, yet we do it anyway, it is only because we have decided not to avail ourselves of that power. We have chosen instead the act of sin, and this choice of our own sinful desires over Christ is, on a smaller scale, just what Judas did.

Therefore, we continue to sin *only because we choose not to claim the promises of God in Christ.* We are choosing sin over Jesus. The Lord can pardon our sins. But if we continue in them we will sooner or later, like Judas, become so hardened in them that we will make the same decision Judas made and reject Jesus totally. A Christian doesn't have to end his life as Judas did in order to have his name blotted out of the book of life. Instead, he can go to church, tithe, pray, even do some good works, and yet be blotted out of the book of life, with Jesus saying, " 'Depart from Me, you who practice lawlessness' " (Matthew 7:23, NKJV).[10]

Sin is a spiritual nerve disease. It desensitizes us to the differences between right and wrong, evil and good, righteousness and unrighteousness. Distinctions are blurred. The more we sin, the less heinous it appears, the more we justify it, and the less sinful it seems. Judas had rationalized his sin, thinking that by betraying the Lord, Jesus would be forced to become King and Ruler. Thus Judas would be credited for "having placed the king on David's throne. And this act would secure to him the first position, next to Christ, in the new kingdom."[11] Sin had so perverted his mind, so desensitized him to the distinction between good and evil, that he actually rationalized his treachery to the point of thinking that it would exalt himself and Christ!

No wonder the Bible warns against those who are "hardened through the deceitfulness of sin" (Hebrews 3:13). We may think that we are saved, that we are Christians, that we are in a right relationship with God, when all along we may be as duped and hardened as Judas.

The history of Christianity proves that not everyone professing the name of Jesus is converted. Believing that they were doing the work of Christ, church leaders burned men, women, and babies at the stake. They made war in the name of Jesus, tortured, pillaged, and raped in the name of Jesus Christ—believing it was all for the glory of God. These servants of Satan were so blinded in sin that they couldn't tell the difference between right and wrong, between sin and righteousness. We must not fool ourselves, either. Just because we haven't burned some "heretic" in the name of Jesus doesn't mean we can't be just as deceived as those who have. Actually, according to the message to Laodicea, many already are. " 'You say, "I am rich, have become wealthy, and have need of nothing"— and do not know that you are wretched, miserable, poor, blind, and naked' " (Revelation 3:17, NKJV).

When God says to the Laodiceans, I will "spue thee out of my mouth" (verse 16), the Greek literally reads, "I will vomit thee out." It doesn't sound as if Laodiceans will be feasting with Jesus at the banquet in heaven, does it? Unless they change, unless they accept the counsel given in the next verse, they will be blotted out of the book of life, even though they are deceived into thinking that they are fine!

"Through defects in the character," Ellen White warns, "Satan works to gain control of the whole mind, and he knows that if these defects are cherished, he will succeed. Therefore he is constantly seeking to deceive the followers of Christ with his fatal sophistry that it is impossible for them to overcome."[12]

In Luke 18, Jesus told of two men praying in the temple, a Pharisee and a tax collector. " 'The Pharisee stood and prayed thus with himself, 'God, I thank You that I am not like other men—extortioners, unjust, adulterers, or even as this tax collector. I fast twice a week; I give tithes of all that I possess' " (verses 11, 12, NKJV). Meanwhile, the tax collector, " 'standing afar off, would not so much as raise his eyes to heaven, but beat his breast, saying, "God be merciful to me a sinner!' " (verse 13, NKJV). Jesus then said that the tax collector, not the Pharisee,

" 'went down to his house justified' " (verse 14, NKJV).

Who was so hardened in sin that he couldn't see his own defects? Who left the temple still in his sins? Who was as duped regarding his true spiritual condition as were the Laodiceans? Of course, the Pharisee. On the other hand, who was living closer to Jesus? Who knew the holiness and perfection that God demanded? Who experienced his absolute need of the righteousness of Christ to cover his sins? Of course, the tax collector.

Our own experience should teach us that the more victories we achieve in Christ, the closer we will come to Jesus, and thus the more sinful and unholy we will appear to ourselves. A person who hadn't sinned in a year would be the last to know it, much less boast about it. Sin separates us from Christ, and the further we are separated from Him, the less clearly we discern our sinful state, and the more likely we are to pray as the Pharisee prayed. Those who get the most victories will beat their breasts the hardest because they will be walking the closest to Jesus, whose righteousness causes them to stand in the shame of their own shortcomings. It's ironic, but the more victories we attain in Christ, the more we will perceive our need of His righteousness.

Ellen White warns that "sins that have not been repented of and forsaken will not be pardoned and blotted out of the books of record, but will stand to witness against the sinner in the day of God."[13] Who was in greater danger of not repenting of his sin—the Pharisee or the tax collector? The Pharisee, but only because he was so deceived by his own sins that he wasn't even aware of them. Sin hardens and blinds all of us to our true spiritual condition. Because we won't repent of and forsake sins that we aren't aware of, those hardened in sin are likely to have unrepented, unforsaken sin to witness against them in the day of judgment.

All who have truly repented of sin, and by faith claimed the blood of Christ as their atoning sacrifice, have had pardon entered against their names in the books of heaven; as they have become partakers of the righteousness of Christ, and their characters are found to be in harmony with the law of God, their sins will be blotted out, and they themselves will be accounted worthy of eternal life.[14]

This isn't salvation by works. A life in harmony with the law of God will not get anyone into heaven. Only a perfect record will save us, and the only Man who ever had that perfect record was Jesus, which is why all need "the blood of Christ as their atoning sacrifice." The characters that we form through the righteousness of Christ give us a life in harmony with the law of God. This is the proof, the outward evidence, that we truly have a saving faith. "Show me your faith without your works," said James, "and I will show you my faith by my works" (James 2:18). The investigative judgment, as a review of our works, determines whether or not we really have exercised true faith.

Jesus Christ promised not only forgiveness of sin, but victory over it as well. Redemption is a package deal. If we have accepted forgiveness, we must accept victory. And those victories testify in the day of judgment that we have truly been redeemed. This is why Ellen White could write: "He who has not sufficient faith in Christ to believe that He can keep him from sinning, has not the faith that will give him an entrance into the kingdom of God."[15]

The investigative judgment reveals to the onlooking universe whether we have truly been saved. Anyone can claim that they are saved, that they are servants of Christ. In the investigative judgment, it is determined for the onlooking universe if such claims are valid. If, living in sinful flesh, facing tremendous temptations, and with the devil riding our backs, we nevertheless choose Jesus over sin here on earth, then in heaven, without sinful flesh, without these temptations, and without a devil breathing down our necks, we certainly won't cause trouble there.

We remain justified by overcoming through the power promised us. Had Judas, through the power of Christ, attained victory over his greed, he would not have abandoned Christ. His name might have remained in the book of life. Sin can separate us from God to the point that we can lose our salvation. Without allowing Christ to uproot the inherited and cultivated evil in our lives, we will fall away.

In Matthew 7, Jesus contrasts two individuals. One hears His words and "doeth them" (verse 24). The other hears His words but "doeth them not" (verse 26). The obedient one, who does what Jesus commands, stays faithful unto the end. "By works was [his] faith made perfect" (James 2:22). The disobedient one, who doesn't do what Jesus commands, falls away. His "faith without works is dead" (James 2:26).

While God can be just, and yet justify the sinner through the merits of Christ, no man can cover his soul with the garments of Christ's righteousness while practicing known sins, or neglecting known duties. God requires the entire surrender of the heart, before justification can take place; and in order for man to retain justification, there must be continual obedience, through active, living faith that works by love and purifies the soul.[16]

This doesn't mean that every time you sin you are out of salvation. Instead, justification is an ongoing process that needs to be cultivated, maintained, and nurtured daily to avoid losing it. "As ye have therefore received Christ Jesus the Lord, so walk . . . in him" (Colossians 2:6). We received Christ by a total surrender of self, and the only way to maintain His presence is by a daily surrender which will result in obedience, growth, and victory. The investigative judgment finally determines whether we have maintained that saving relationship.

The investigative judgment is not the time when God finally decides to accept or abandon us. All those written in heaven have already been accepted by God. Instead, the judgment merely finalizes our choice to keep or reject Him. The judgment is where *our decisions* are sealed one way or another.

But some say that the investigative judgment robs them of assurance. How much assurance do they want? If they want absolute assurance that once they accept Jesus they can never be lost, they should join a church that teaches "once saved, always saved." If, however, we daily surrender our lives to Jesus, praising Him for the victories we receive, repenting and forsaking sin when we fall, relying totally on the merits of Christ imputed to us as

177

our only hope of salvation, then we will have all the assurance we need. Anything promised beyond that is presumption.

Works do not save us. They cannot save us and are not meant to save us. But that does not mean they have nothing to do with salvation. On the contrary, they are the proof, the evidence, that we have been saved. If we are truly converted, our works will testify to it, and we will have nothing to fear in the judgment.

Some ask, How will I know if I have enough works to be saved? The answer is easy. You don't have enough works to be saved, and you never will. That is why we need Jesus covering us with His righteousness. All we can do is lean on Him, plead His merits on our behalf, and trust that He is a righteous, compassionate Judge who will judge us according to His infinite wisdom and mercy.

What more do we need?

1. *The Desire of Ages*, p. 717.
2. Ibid.
3. *Christ's Object Lessons*, p. 310.
4. *The Desire of Ages*, p. 717.
5. Ibid., p. 716.
6. Ibid., p. 720.
7. *Review and Herald*, Sept. 4, 1883.
8. *The Ministry of Healing*, p. 180.
9. *The Great Controversy*, p. 582.
10.The NKVJ translation of this verse is quite accurate. The word translated "iniquity" in the KJV is literally *anomia*, meaning, "without the law" or "lawlessness."
11. *The Desire of Ages*, p. 721.
12. *The Great Controversy*, p. 489.
13. Ibid., p. 486.
14. Ibid., p. 483.
15. *Selected Messages*, bk. 3, p. 360.
16. *Selected Messages*, bk. 1, p. 366.

Chapter **18**

# The Judas in All of Us (Cont.)

T here is, however, a little Judas in all of us. Many of us love Jesus, love this message, love this church, and want to be saved, yet sin still clings to us, or rather, we still cling to sin. What, then, is the key to overcoming? How can we be numbered among those named in Revelation: "He who overcomes shall be clothed in white garments, and I will not blot out his name from the Book of Life; but I will confess his name before My Father and before His angels" (Revelation 3:5, NKJV).

Some teach that we need to pray a certain way, and then we will overcome. No doubt, prayer is important. Without it, we don't have a prayer of a chance. Others stress morning devotions because these will establish for us a relationship with Jesus. It's true that without knowing Jesus, we will never overcome. For some, the key to victory is to minister, to work for the salvation of souls, and to witness.

All these factors are important. But did Judas pray, minister, and have a relationship with Jesus? Of course. Yet what happened to him? How many of us, too, pray, have devotions, witness, and still fall into sin? Obviously, more is needed.

We can pray, have a consistent devotional life, and witness, yet unless we are willing to apply one principle in our walk with the Lord, we will *be overcome by sin* rather than overcome it. When we apply this principle, God will never fail us; when we don't, we will always fail God.

"Forasmuch then as Christ hath suffered for us in the flesh, arm yourselves likewise with the same mind: for he that hath suffered in the flesh hath ceased from sin" (1 Peter 4:1).

What does it mean that Christ has suffered for us in the flesh? Peter is not talking primarily about Calvary because the Saviour's sufferings on the Cross were more spiritual than physical. The spikes in His hands didn't kill Him; the sins of the world did.

How then did Christ suffer for us in the flesh? What about the forty days and nights fasting in the wilderness, where He won the victory for us over appetite, presumption, and the desire for worldly glory? Did He not suffer for us in the flesh there, gaining victories that we can share? Of course. What about His whole life in which He was "tempted like as we are, yet without sin" (Hebrews 4:15)? Didn't these temptations cause Him to suffer? "It was fitting for Him, for whom are all things . . . in bringing many sons to glory, to make the author of their salvation perfect through sufferings" (Hebrews 2:10, NKJV). "Though He was a Son, yet He learned obedience by the things which He suffered" (Hebrews 5:8, NKJV).

Jesus was a human being, with human flesh that craved fulfillment the same way we crave it, and the only way He could have endured the onslaughts of the devil was to be willing to suffer in the flesh to gain victory over sin through the power of God. That is the only way we can overcome as well.

Pray, have devotions, witness, but when the devil is pressing you, when every cell of your body cries out for sin, when your hormones, appetites, and passions steam through your pores—all you can do is claim God's promises for victory and grasp them in cold, naked faith. You will have terrible moments of agony, your nerves will be stretched on end, and you'll think you are dying. Then, just when you can't stand it anymore, the temptation will pass, and through the power of Jesus, and to His honor and glory, you will rejoice in your victories through the Lord, "who is able to keep you from falling."

Nothing else works. If we're falling, it is because we are not suffering in the flesh in order to stand. It's so much easier to succumb, though each time we do, it gets harder to resist the next time. Before long, without even knowing it, we are as much under the control of Satan as was Judas.

Ellen White wrote about her struggle to overcome an addiction to a type of vinegar:

> For weeks I was very sick; but I kept saying over and over, The Lord knows all about it. If I die, I die;

but I will not yield to this desire. The struggle continued, and I was sorely afflicted for many weeks.
All thought that it was impossible for me to live. You
may be sure we sought the Lord very earnestly. The
most fervent prayers were offered for my recovery. I
continued to resist the desire for vinegar, and at last
I conquered. Now I have no inclination to taste anything of the kind. This experience has been of great
value to me in many ways. I obtained a complete
victory.[1]

Was this salvation by works? Was Ellen White a legalist? Will she be accepted into heaven because she was
victorious over vinegar? Of course not. What she experienced exemplified suffering in the flesh in order to obtain
victories in Jesus.

When was the last time you heard in Adventism of anyone suffering like this to obtain a victory? Why, this would
be called legalism! Some would say that Ellen White didn't
need to suffer so. She should have drunk the vinegar all
she wanted. In God's time, He'd give her the victory. Until
then, her struggles were merely salvation by works.

Such cruel trials and struggles are not legalism. They
are, in reality, the way we claim and receive Christ's
promises of victory, despite the misery and pain. "For he
that hath suffered in the flesh hath ceased from sin."
Suffering in the flesh means just that: suffering. If we will
not suffer in the flesh in order to overcome our sins, we
will die in them instead.

Some sins, the moment we accept Jesus, disappear;
others cling so close to our souls they seem wrapped in
the molecules of our DNA. It feels easier to tear out our

hearts than to give them up. Nevertheless, we must, and Jesus promises success.

Nothing is apparently more helpless, yet really more invincible, than the soul that feels its nothingness and relies wholly on the merits of the Saviour. God would send every angel in heaven to the aid of such a one, rather than allow him to be overcome.[2]

What a promise! Yet even with legions of winged beings hovering by our side, unless we choose to suffer in the flesh to overcome the clamors over our fallen natures, unless we choose not to sin no matter the agonizing within us, we will not "cease from sin," and sin will destroy us. Satan will use sin so to control our minds that we will not see our need of pardon, and unforsaken, unconfessed sin will stand against us in the day of judgment. Or we will be driven to despair and give up on Jesus totally.

Yet, God can make a way of escape. Had Judas been willing to suffer in the flesh, had he in the name and power of Jesus sought the victories that Jesus wanted to give him, he would be rising with the redeemed. Instead, he will burn with the damned.

God didn't abandon Judas. Judas abandoned Him. God won't abandon us. But the question is, Will we abandon Him? Every day, by the choices we make, by the victories we either choose to gain or forfeit, we are answering that question. The choices we make—either for good or evil—will one day be forever fixed in the judgment.

---

1. *Counsels on Diet and Foods,* p. 485.
2. *Testimonies for the Church,* vol. 7, p. 17.

# Chapter 19

# False Balances

**W**hen I meet new Adventists, I give two pieces of advice.

First: *Trust no one.* I don't mean that you can't love people, learn from them, or respect them. Instead, we need to be grounded in truth, we need to know for ourselves what we believe, and then stick to it no matter what anyone—even the one who brought you into this message—says or does. Often, we will admire someone, who then kicks a dog or does something that dashes our faith, and, disappointed, we step back. Step back now. Be firm in present truth by leaning on Jesus alone.

You can listen, learn from people, love them, but train yourself to weigh every human word against God's Word. No matter who the person is, how smart or holy he appears, or how much influence he has had on your life, you must stand alone. Those whom I have loved or admired the most have sometimes disappointed me the worst; some have even gone off the deep end and, had I not cut the cords, I could have gone off with them. We don't know what lurks within each other's hearts. We don't need to. Instead, we need to know Jesus and His truth for this time. Nothing else, no one else, will work. " 'Though these three men, Noah, Daniel, and Job, were in it [the land], they would deliver only themselves by their righteousness,' says the Lord God" (Ezekiel 14:14, NKJV).

The other point I stress is: *balance, balance, balance.* Every aspect of this message without exception, exemption, or deviation must be kept in proper balance, or you will drift into heresy, fanaticism, or nonsense. Most heresy battering the church today, as in the past, results from an *imbalance* of truth. The devil rarely brings in total error. He knows he can work much better and catch more people if he can arrange for an element of truth to be so emphasized that other important elements are neglected until they become almost meaningless. By far, imbalance forms the root of most error within Adventism today, particularly in regard to righteousness by faith and the final generation.

In years past, many Adventists were apparently not taught a balanced understanding of the sanctuary. They got the second apartment alone: law, obedience, perfection, victory over sin. A whole generation seemed clouded in a miasma of guilt.

As a result, certain teachers and preachers (many of whom suffered from the same problem) sought to help these people by emphasizing the legal, forensic aspect of the cross. The Adventist Church needed the corrective focus. What we are seeing today, however, is an equally devastating imbalance. Instead of balancing the law, obedience, and victory with the cross, we have so emphasized forensic justification that victory, character development, and obedience to the law are becoming mere footnotes to the gospel. None teaches outright disobedience; instead, some teach that we can be saved in spite of disobedience. Jesus declares you righteous, they tell us, but He can't make you so. We can never stop sinning, and it doesn't really affect our salvation anyway because Jesus covered it all by dying on the cross. With such an unbalanced presentation of the sanctuary, with all the emphasis on the altar of burnt offering and the first apartment, no wonder that the rest of the sanctuary service, especially the second apartment ministry and the investigative judgment, has been clouded, even lost. If the gospel is what Christ has done for us on the cross alone, who needs an investigative judgment?

As such teachings have spread, others have overreacted. Instead of balancing forensic justification, they have rejected it totally, reverting so much into the law, overcoming, and obedience that they have drifted into legalism and rank perfectionism. (Perfectionism is not character perfection. Perfectionism teaches that we become perfect and that this perfection is what saves us.) These individuals can't accept that we are saved 100 percent by what Jesus has done outside of us, in place of us, and for us. Their whole theology is experiential; what Christ does in us is alone the basis of our salvation. They pay lip service to justification, claim they believe it, but deep down they don't accept it any more than those on the other side accept the investigative judgment.

187

As a result of this imbalance, those who teach the forensic-only aspect of the gospel have gone even further, coming up with a cheap grace that is worthless. Meanwhile, the legalists, overreacting to this overreaction, go further into legalism. Each side continually overreacts to the other, until both are steeped in error. This results in strange teachings from the left and the right.

The far-left-wingers tell us that the law cannot be kept, that we will always be sinning, and that therefore it doesn't matter if we sin after probation closes because it's over, and those sins will not be transferred into the heavenly sanctuary. God, apparently, just shrugs these sins off. For these individuals, Ellen White's statements about character perfection don't really mean what they say and, besides, in her early days, she was more of a legalist than in her later years. Later in her life (they claim), she didn't teach the character perfection of the final generation. Ultimately, these individuals cannot accept the investigative judgment. Ellen White and the pioneers, they believe, were simply wrong; judgment took place at the cross. They constantly harp on the beast of legalism. And though legalism has certainly been prevalent in the church, with the drop in our standards, with increasing drug and alcohol use, with rising sexual promiscuity among our members, with skyrocketing divorce, and with financial and sexual scandals within the church—somehow, legalism doesn't seem to be our problem!

The far-right-wingers earnestly stress, teach, and preach perfection. They always have quotes about perfection to beat over the heads of the liberals, though these people can be the nastiest, most judgmental, and unloving saints within Adventism. They tend to prejudge your salvation by whether or not you have *their* understanding of the nature of Christ. If you don't measure up, forget it! You might as well be a Jesuit. Some teach that each time you sin, you are out of salvation; others have extreme views of the final generation. Some claim that once probation closes, we will have to stand in our own righteousness, not having Christ's covering anymore. Some believe that we will be so perfect we won't even need the Holy Spirit; that we will be so close to God, so aware of what His will is, that we can be perfect on our own. Some preach that the final generation actually forms an "atonement" for sin that Jesus hasn't accomplished at the cross or in the heavenly sanctuary. For these individuals, salvation is exclusively what Christ does in us, and those who believe in forensic justification as the basis of salvation are into "new theology."

Both sides are in error. Meanwhile, those who don't know what to believe, particularly new Adventists, often get sucked into one camp or another. Don't go to either. If you read your Bible, if you read the Spirit of Prophecy and test everything by them, you will find the balance (as have thousands of Adventists), and a balance is what we need.

As a church, we haven't learned that you don't fight cheap grace with legalism. You fight cheap grace by getting rid of the cheapness, not the grace. And you don't fight legalism by downplaying, denigrating, or nullifying the law. You get rid of the *ism*. We have lost this balance, and until we regain it, we will be fighting among ourselves, hurting our church, and bringing reproach upon the God whom we profess to serve.

The key, however, to this balance is the sanctuary, and

two points are clearly taught from it. First, our only hope in the judgment is that a Substitute will stand in our place and plead His perfect righteousness in our behalf. Second, the day we see that Substitute as an excuse not to be "perfecting holiness in the fear of God" (2 Corinthians 7:1) is the day we slide toward perdition.

This is the gospel. Anyone telling you differently is telling you half the story, and accepting half the story has been, and still is, our problem as a church. It gives us a false balance, and "a false balance is abomination to the Lord" (Proverbs 11:1).

"A just weight," however, "is His delight," and in no area do we need more just weight than in understanding the relationship between the law and grace, especially in regard to the final generation. Nowhere is this just weight revealed better than by the sanctuary service, *the entire service,* from the altar of burnt offerings to the Ten Commandments.

Meanwhile, those who stress one aspect of the gospel at the expense of the other might themselves be found wanting on the day when they are weighed in the balances of the sanctuary. Unless we are hardened and blinded in our sins, world events should warn us that the day is coming soon.